SOLITARY PLEASURES

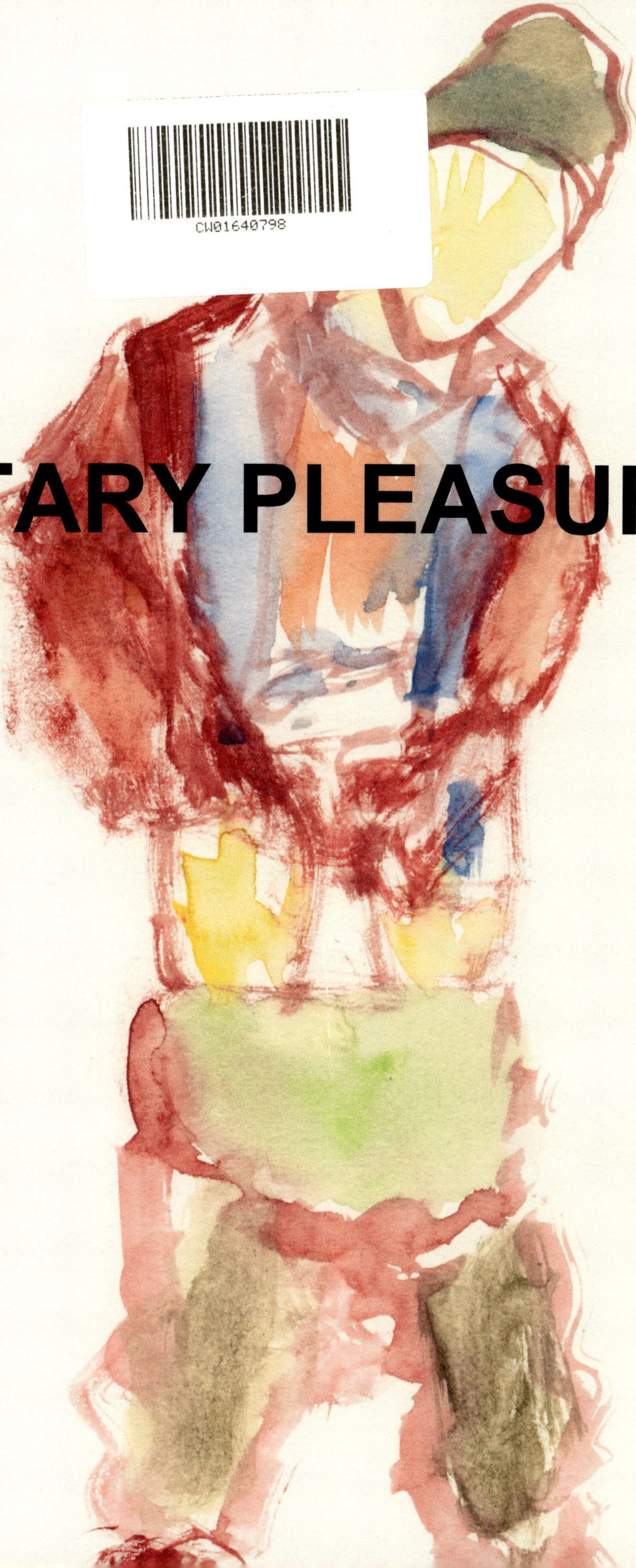

First published in 2018 to coincide with the exhibition *Solitary Pleasures* at the Freud Museum, London, April-May 2018 curated by Marquard Smith

Publication edited by Marquard Smith
Design by Mark Little

Live Art Development Agency (LADA)
The Garrett Centre, 117A Mansford Street, London E2 6LX
www.thisisLiveArt.co.uk

ISBN: 978-0-9935611-6-0

LADA
Live Art
Development
Agency

The Live Art Development Agency (LADA) is a Centre for Live Art: a research and knowledge centre, a production centre for programmes and publications, and an online centre for representation and dissemination. LADA is funded as a National Portfolio Organisation by Arts Council England.

Cover image: Chantal Faust, *Float,* 2003-2018
Frontispiece: Chantal Faust, *Boy Masturbating*, 2016

Preface

Lois Keidan, Live Art Development Agency

The Live Art Development Agency (LADA) is delighted to have collaborated with Marquard Smith as the publisher of *Solitary Pleasures*, a beautiful collection of words and images created to accompany the *Solitary Pleasures* exhibition at the Freud Museum, London in Spring 2018.

There are of course all kinds of connections between the solitary pleasures this project celebrates and the performance art practices LADA supports, not least because so many performance artists have been called wankers over the years. And quite a few of them are indeed wankers - not necessarily in the pejorative sense that might have been intended, but because their art has literally involved them masturbating. From Vito Acconci's *Seedbed* (1972) (re-performed by Marina Abramovic in 2005 as part of *Seven Easy Pieces)* through to Annie Sprinkle's *Post-Porn Modernist* show in the late 1980s and 1990s, Ron Athey's *Joyce* (2002), Kim Noble's *Kim Noble Will Die* (2009) and Jordan McKenzie's *Spent* (2009), a host of artists working with embodied, performance-based practices have engaged with the act, the aesthetics and the politics of ejaculation and the masturbatory, exploring the solitary pleasure of wanking as a generative force, and the potential for an implicitly individual act to be reimagined for collective consumption.

Bodily functions have always distinguished much performance art. There is a rich lineage and proud tradition of artists working with their blood, their piss, their shit, their sweat, their tears, their milk, their mucus, and their semen, whether as signifiers of identity and being, or as markers of fragility and illness, or as modes of protest and resistance to societal norms. And through such embodied actions artists have not only tested the limits of the material body itself, but have opened up different kinds of engagement with the human form and all its difficulties, desires, fluids, and functions.

Much of this kind of performance-based art has, for many years, been seen as marginal, subversive, and transgressive by the dominant culture, so we very much welcome *Solitary Pleasures* as a project which frames these practices within the wider cultural context of extraordinary artists, writers and thinkers who have invited us to consider the aesthetics and cultural value of masturbation differently, which legitimizes counter-hegemonic approaches to being in the world, and which offers alternative ways of imagining our futures.

Introduction: Towards a Divergence Untold

Marquard Smith

Solitary Pleasures is a secret museum, a treasure trove of insightful and delightful drawings, sculptures, photographs, video stills, artefacts, performative gestures, and ephemera – as well as specially commissioned texts by artists, academics, educators, and critical writers – on a subject at the heart of Freudian and post-Freudian sexuality, eroticism, and desire: masturbation.

The premise of *Solitary Pleasures* is that as an act masturbation is all-inclusive; it's gay, lesbian, nonbinary, heterosexual, bisexual, trans, queer, +, +, and +. It's universal and particular, reciprocal and personalised; a solitary pleasure, a shared exchange, an intimate encounter – with ourselves, and between couples, lovers, and strangers. It's also the great leveller, and as such is crucial to making sense, in one way or another, of all of us as human beings and as sexual beings, of human sexuality and of our own true sexual selves.

Big claims, and tough to orchestrate, but no one said it would be easy-peasy.

First off, *Solitary Pleasures* looks to detail masturbation's unique aesthetic, barely scrutinised until now, and does so by way of work and words from awesome contributors Shannon Bell, Lee Edelman, VALIE EXPORT, Chantal Faust, Sigmund Freud, Antony Gormley, Dominic Johnson, Lois Keidan, Wayne Koestenbaum, Thomas W. Laqueur, Jordan McKenzie, Susie Orbach, Emily Pope, Adrian Rifkin, Charan Singh, Beth Stephens & Annie Sprinkle, Emma Talbot, Cosey Fanni Tutti, Ivan Ward, and Michelle Williams Gamaker. Through these works and words, the contributors delineate, observe, and honour - thereby composing - this aesthetic as at once graphic, material, and embodied; politically affirmative and ethically unclear; joyful and ejaculatory; comforting and confrontational; sensuous and inhuman; theatrical and performative; fictive, phantasmagorical, phantasmatic; parodic and farcical; repetitive, pained, banal; and desolate, desperate, and heart-rending.

We diverge and we amass models and modalities of masturbation.

Because masturbation is their source and origin, together this cacophony of works and words makes manifest, extends, and challenges more familiar, normative conceptualisations of sexuality, eroticism, perversity, touching, intimacy, frustration, and gratification. Individually and collectively, the contributions do this by drawing (explicitly and implicitly) on the history of masturbation in which this 'solitary pleasure' has been figured in various ways, including as a disorder, as 'unnatural' and 'unhealthy', and as a violation of the moral law, *and,* conversely, as a vital force, as a creative and magical act, and as 'normal' and 'healthy'. It is dangerous *to* masturbate, and dangerous *not to* masturbate! Riding these contradictions without ever wanting to resolve them, in this publication overall we draw out and critically interrogate how masturbation as a proposition can transform our understanding of such deeply complex terms as they are woven into Freudian and post-Freudian considerations of the human subject, human subjectivity, and human sexuality.

In *Solitary Pleasures* the contributors lay bare how and why - historically, conceptually, and aesthetically - masturbation is dangerous. Whether understood as a 'solitary vice', a 'solitary pleasure', or, as we propose, as an act or series of acts that are much more diverging and amassing than either, what fascinates is the different (and often conflicting) reasons why it is dangerous.

Socially, ideologically, psycho-sexually, masturbation is dangerous because, as historian Thomas Laqueur has argued, historically it has been considered a 'fundamentally asocial or socially degenerate practice' in which 'healthy desire' is channelled back into itself rather than into the regulative hetero-normativity of socially productive forms of heterosexual intercourse.(1) That is to say, its dangerous-ness comes in the first instance from the fact it is a practice that can and is enacted (whether alone or in company) in and of itself rather than as an encounter on the path to procreation. Mere touching is itself a danger, and even a perversion, warned Sigmund Freud in his *Three Essays on the Theory of Sexuality* in 1905, if the individual becomes preoccupied by 'lingering over the stage of touching' at the expense of and to the extent that the (so called normal) 'sexual act' is no longer the desired outcome of any given encounter.(2) As an instance of fore-pleasure, in *not* culminating in the sexual act proper, or end-pleasure, masturbation is thus dangerous because as an 'inadequate' form of sexual activity it supposedly short-circuits desire and fulfilment. It is dangerous *because it is a practice that is productive of pleasure in and of itself and as an end in itself*, rather than as a means to a reproductive end.

We speak on behalf of short-circuiting such normative desire and fulfilment.

With necessary and express consent as a non-negotiable hard limit, as active agents we entertain masturbation's asociality as well as its sociality; the distinctiveness of its pleasures and its un-pleasures; its ordinary-ness and unconventionality; its libidinal economy and will-to-death; its sadism and masochism and sado-masochism; its narcissism and self-satisfying;

its bleakness; and its inadequate, lingering, non-procreative intimacies. We entertain these structures of feeling, and we welcome how these pleasures (and frustrations) in and of themselves, and as ends in themselves, as practices or acts enact both the fact of vital, embodied, material encounters with ourselves and with others, *and* dare to cultivate flights of imaginative phantasy.

Such an entertaining is necessary to extricate ourselves and each other from the shackles of early capitalism's insidious monopolisation of the erotic; a subjectification that assumed a certain fervour with the invention of the anti-masturbation industry over 300 years ago in which masturbation is exhaustively formalised as a danger in the catchily-titled *Onania: or, the Heinous Sin of Self-Pollution, and all its Frightful Consequences (in Both Sexes) Considered: With Spiritual and Phyfical Advice to thofe who have already injured themfelves by this abominable Practice*, published around 1712.

This anti-onanistic sentiment sows the seeds for masturbation's lingering as a danger, as sinful, self-polluting, injurious, abominable, but also, as I've already intimated, because of the extent to which it is aeconomical; and this is why its danger persists and perhaps even intensifies in our own neo-liberal semio-capitalist condition. For masturbation is constitutively and radically against the economy of heterosexual genital intercourse. It is 'that dangerous supplement' deceiving 'nature' – because it supplants rather than complements nature – and thus the natural order of things. It is non-procreative eroticism. And thus eroticism as such. Desire unleashed. Against classical utility, masturbation is generative and non-generative, productive and disposable, a perverse sexuality that speaks of a non-genital finality, a matter of 'non-logical difference'. As symptomatic of Georges Bataille's general economy, it is unproductive expenditure par excellence.

Supposedly unproductive activities always lead, and are tied to economic anxieties. And masturbation is an autarky: economically self-reliant and self-sufficient. Because of this, it is today and for the foreseeable future a raging ungovernable nuisance for our quantitative milieu, for bureaucratic regimes, for the accountants, the bean counters. Keep counting, fuckers! Because masturbation is no economy of scarcity. It defies paucity, says no to bare life, to just-getting-by. As Laqueur writes, there is no bottom line in the masturbatory economy (Laqueur, 2003, p. 290). You come, come, and come again. Gushing. Spurting. Trickling. Spasming. Shuddering. Quivering. Tingling. Cathecting. Ripples or crashing wave after wave after wave of release, of relief. And even if maybe there's no release, even if there's just desire frustrated, desire dashed, this is itself a surfeit of *sensation-ing* too. Fiscally-speaking, in our global economy especially, and against the vile coercive tendencies of emotional capitalism and the capitalism-ization and real subsumption of the erotic, and of desire, if ever there is an activity to participate in that's anti-capitalist, masturbation is it!

Masturbation is a challenge (and a danger) to the already crumbling edifice of 'heterosexuality' because also it draws attention to the fact that the 'normative' in hetero-normativity is itself perverse. That's to say, let's be reminded that the majority of practices designated historically as intrinsically perverse because they're non-productive activities that 'deviate' from the path to (and don't culminate in) breeding (masturbation, fetishism, sodomy, bestiality, Pygmalionism, and so on, even simple foreplay), are *the very practices* forming the taxonomy of perversions that 'invent' heterosexuality as *itself* polymorphously perverse. Thus masturbation as a heterosexual (as well as as gay, lesbian, nonbinary, bisexual, trans, queer, +, +, and +) practice, because it is integral to the structure and economy of the hetero-normative *also* promises the staging of a critique of that system; even *it* works against the classical utility of the economy of heterosexual genital intercourse, and *for* non-productive forms of generation.

Solitary Pleasures proposes also that with masturbation as a remarkably elusive and contradictory starting point, we can observe how 'civilizing' as a process shapes, transforms, expresses, and enforces notions of human sexuality and our sexual selves. In this respect, it is a cornerstone upon which can be built our sense of *contemporary relations* between human beings, sexuality, and intimacy. That is to say, such contemporary relations are being configured today by familiar and unfamiliar factors, not least by technology. (Here I refer to both technology per se, but also to how Michel Foucault defined technologies of the self: those practices through which we constitute ourselves as human subjects, our relations to ourselves, to one another, and to the world.) Since our emotional lives are nowadays created, navigated, and performed *through* technology and as technology, such relations between human beings, sexuality, and intimacy must then take account of for instance online pornography, 'loveless sex', virtual partners, online dating, geosocial networking, and our erotomanic relations with non-sentient forms (dolls, vibrators, computer operating systems, and so forth); what German Sexologist Iwan Bloch all those years ago referred to as 'foreign bodies and objects'.(4)

(Given our devotion to technology, it is worth noting that in a letter to Wilhelm Fliess in 1897 Freud described masturbation as 'the primary addition', to which later addictions such as alcohol, tobacco, and morphine are substitutes. Masturbation is thus constitutive and institutive of all addictions, a detail to keep in mind every time you reach for your iPhone.)(5)

Masturbation as a technology of the self can thus pinpoint the persistence (as well as the changing nature) of our craving to establish relations to ourselves, to other human beings, and to inanimate human forms in ways that are often figured as intimate, empathetic, and reciprocal. Such efforts betray a further (and menacing) danger of masturbation, certainly in its hetero-normative forms as they permeate non-hetero-normative spheres, behaviours, and sentiments: it has the potential to *confuse* distinctive relations to ourselves, between persons and persons, and persons and things that lead to alienation and reification of the self, and estrangement from others.(6)

Confirming and confounding Freud and post-Freudian thought, for good and ill masturbation becomes not only a *substitute* for 'proper' relations between human beings, and to ourselves, but, fascinatingly and oftentimes disturbingly, perhaps even a *model for actual sex*.

One version of masturbation as a model for actual sex - the most familiar, at least in the popular imagination - is the pathetic figure of the lone hetero-masculine man (alone, but multiplied millions and millions of times globally), in the privacy of his own home (unless he's still living with his parents), sat in front of his computer screen, watching internet porn, and jerking off. A direct descendent of the sinners, self-polluters, the injured, and the abominable populating *Onania* from around 1712, he is, the literature tells us, either filled with self-loathing and shame-fueled anger, liberated from the un-fulfill-able expectations of burdensome relationships, or a combination of the two. He may well just be enjoying himself of course, but it's more likely that, even if that's true, as a figure he'll still get caught up in the excitable speech around (sexual) health and well being vis-à-vis feelings of loneliness and social inadequacy on the one hand, or, on the other, discourse on the profound narcissism of toxic masculinity.(7)

Most recently, a more predatory variant of this version of masturbation as a model for actual sex has been given heightened visibility, with revelations around numerous high profile individuals accused of sexual harassment, sexual exploiting, and sexual misconduct, including rape. Film producer Harvey Weinstein is joined by photographers Terry Richardson and Mario Testino, comedian Louis CK, film director James Toback, and others, and many of the accusations directed at them include acts not unrelated to the matter at hand. Subject to unwanted advances in general, specifically these men often allegedly asked or demanded that their employees, colleagues, or friends, both men and women, watch them masturbate. (The actor Selma Blair for one relays that Toback insisted she let him pleasure himself in front of her.)(8) Rather than the pathetic solitary male sat in front of his computer, this is the predatory Weinstein et al sat in front of his people jerking off. Here masturbation is no longer a solitary pleasure (or vice for that matter) but rather a semi-social (albeit anti-social) act, an abuse of power performed in a private setting for semi-public consumption to a non-consenting audience. I am certainly not the one to make an argument, here or anywhere else, for such acts as evidence of masturbation as a model for actual sex that, because of its intrinsic dangerous-ness, works against the economy of heterosexual genital intercourse thereby providing a critique of hetero-normative culture. No, we don't need that. And for the record, we must register such coercive acts as instances of masturbation as a model for actual sex, interrogate them, call out and rage against the offenders, mock them by all means, and confront and challenge, day in and day out, the values and behaviors of such hetero-masculinist sexual entitlement.

That said, even in the midst of our post-Weinstein #MeToo, Time's Up moment, in fact actively against what spawned it, what we must at the same time do is discern, render, and endorse other, preferable, *better* variants of masturbation as a model for actual sex; they must all come to the fore. It is beholden on us to diverge and amass models and modalities of masturbation.

'We are all agreed on one thing – that the subject of masturbation is quite inexhaustible'. This is how Freud would conclude a discussion on masturbation held at the Vienna Psychoanalytic Society in 1912, around 200 years after the publication of *Onania*, the tome that ushered in the anti-masturbatory industry. Over 100 years after Freud's statement, the subject continues to be a quite inexhaustible one, albeit one that has become somewhat monopolized by finite figures and restrictive forms, and through *Solitary Pleasures* we hope to keep the conversation going, by willing it to enter a new phase.

For masturbation, as I've declared more than once, is always there, for good and ill – because it's dangerous and thus doubled-edged and Janus-faced - as a barometer to gauge, designate and stress what's significant about where we're at vis-à-vis the human subject, human subjectivity, and human sexuality.

And, in *Solitary Pleasures*, we want to claim masturbation for the good; as a way of making sense of our relations to ourselves, and to each other, that's more… affirmative.

So we diverge and we amass.

Because we believe that masturbation – aesthetically, conceptually, and as an act or series of acts – offers innumerable affirmations, and does so with some urgency: that it might mark empowerment and social justice; defiance and non-compliance; counter-hegemony and dissensus; a promise of the right to live and to love and to lust, to assert the force of a desire, of what one wants; of a pleasure, of an erotic act or encounter that might bring about change; of a frustration, an exasperation and infuriation that might do likewise. Masturbation as a model for actual sex is diversifying and amassing, and, well, fun! It's the beginning of a conversation, *a good conversation,* that might be... ongoing.

In *Solitary Pleasures*, we affirm masturbation's aesthetic – that is constituted and made anew here by way of these works and words – as social and sexual hieroglyphs, a lexicon, a rhetoric, a sonic-auditory domain, a tactile topography, an aromatic and flavoursome feast, a veritable realm of and for the senses that is becoming discernable; if only we attend to the human capacity, *our capacity* to take heed. For these works and words advance new models and modalities for us to scrutinise and seek out, enliven exhausted ones, and provide a glut of facts and fictions and counter-factuals, some inexplicable and bewildering, all of which might lead to unanticipated marvelousness.

We diverge and amass masturbation's models and modalities for actual sex, and this is how solitary pleasures become pleasures shared.

As an interrogation and celebration of all things masturbatory, *Solitary Pleasures* is a wonderfully wondrous cabinet of curiosities for every he, she, and they seriously and actively interested in sexuality, eroticism, desire, narcissism, perversity, intimacy, frustration, and gratification. We celebrate masturbation as a 'solitary pleasure' (not a 'solitary vice') and also as a pleasure that's for everyone, each and every one of us alone and together. As an affirmative, shared, intimate encounter with ourselves, and between couples, lovers, and strangers, masturbation really does re-define desire's and eroticism's possibilities.(9)

Endnotes

1. Thomas Laqueur (1992) *Making Sex: Body and Gender from the Greeks to Freud*, Cambridge, Mass: Harvard University Press, p. 229, and Thomas W. Laqueur (2003) *Solitary Sex: A Cultural History of Masturbation*, New York: Zone Books. On masturbation (and on secret museums) see also Murat Aydemir (2007) *Images of Bliss: Ejaculation, Masculinity, Meaning*, Minneapolis: University of Minnesota Press; Paula Bennett and Vernon A. Rossario II, eds. (1995) *Solitary Pleasures: The Historical, Literary, and Artistic Discourses of Autoeroticism*, London: Routledge; Leo Bersani (1995) *Homos*, Cambridge, Mass: Harvard University Press; Gilles Deleuze (1991) *Coldness and Cruelty*, New York: Zone Books; Jacques Derrida (1976[1967]) *Of Grammatology*, trans. Gayatri Chakravorty Spivak, Baltimore: Johns Hopkins University Press; Mels van Driel (2012) *With the Hand: A Cultural History of Masturbation*, trans. by Paul Vincent, London: Reaktion Books; Sigmund Freud, passim; Michael Grant (1982) *Eros in Pompeii: The Secret Rooms of the National Museum of Naples*, New York: Bonanza Books; Luce Irigaray (1985[1977]) 'This Sex

Which Is Not One,' in *The Sex Which Is Not One*, trans. by Catherine Porter with Carolyn Burke, Ithaca: Cornell University Press, pp. 23-33; Diane Mason (2008) *The Secret Vice: Masturbation in Victorian Fiction and Medical Culture*, Manchester: Manchester University Press; and Marina Wallace, Martin Kemp, and Joanne Bernstein (2007) *Seduced: Art & Sex from Antiquity to Now*, London: Merrell/Barbican.

2. For Freud seeing, usually understood as the nexus of perversity, is an activity that is ultimately derived from touching. See Sigmund Freud, *Three Essays on the Theory of Sexuality*, in Sigmund Freud, *On Sexuality*, Harmondsworth: Pelican Books, pp. 33-169.

3.See Marquard Smith (2014) *The Erotic Doll: A Modern Fetish*: London: Yale University Press.

4. See Iwan Bloch (1908) *The Sexual Life of Our Time in its Relations to Modern Civilization*, London: Heinemann, pp. 411–13. Even in just the last few years, the ways of figuring intimate and erotic relations between humans and non-human forms (which are often erotic, sexual, and masturbatory) has witnessed a significant shift. This is most easily evidenced in the transition from Ryan Gosling's character in Craig Gillespie's *Lars and the Real Girl* (2007) who falls in love with a sex doll (material, synthetic, an object of projected fantasy, faithful, etc.) to Joachin Phoenix's character in Spike Jonze's *Her* (2013) who falls in love with an intelligent computer operating system (immaterial, bio-computational, artificial intelligence, autonomous, unfaithful, etc.)

5. See Sigmund Freud (1985) *The Complete Letters of Sigmund Freud to Willelm Fliess 1887-1904*, trans. by J.F. Masson, Cambridge: Harvard University Press, p. 187.

6. This is of course a continuation of the argument of the convergence in modernity of Freud's appraisal of perversion and Marx's of capitalism and the commodity form. A couple of examples on masturbation as an alienating technology of the self: (1) for Luce Irigaray, auto-affection for men always already involves some kind of mediation by way of a tool or an instrument: a hand, a device, a woman's body. Here, because of this enforced distance that he has from himself while touching himself, he can only touch himself as other to himself. Contrary to this, as Irigaray makes clear, woman's masturbation needs no mediation. She touches herself 'in and of herself.' See Luce Irigaray (1985[1977]), p. 24; and see also Kelly Dennis, 'Playing with Herself: Feminine Sexuality and Aesthetic Indifference', in Paula Bennett and Vernon A. Rossario II, eds. (1995), pp. 49-72, p. 65. (2) Leo Bersani, always ready to push things a little further, suggests that the authority lies elsewhere since for him 'in masturbation the... body, more specifically the penis, disciplines the hand that would rule it.' See Leo Bersani (1995) *Homos*, Cambridge, Mass: Harvard University Press. See also Adrian Rifkin (2010) 'Apart from Sex', *Journal of Visual Culture*, 8:3, pp. 265–277.

7. It is this figure - or figures like him - that is a key character in 'Incel' (involuntary celibate) culture for 'people who lack romantic relationships and sex' and is populated by men whose feelings of sexual isolation are combined directly with generating content that encourages and glorifies violence and rape. Neither benign nor paltry, the Incel group that was recently closed down on Reddit had 40,000 members. See Amia Srinivasan (2018) 'Does anyone have the right to sex?', *London Review of Books*, 22nd March, pp. 5-10.

8. https://www.theguardian.com/film/2017/oct/26/selma-blair-james-toback-threatened-to-kill-me-after-sexual-harassment

9. In finalising *Solitary Pleasures* – both this publication and the exhibition that accompanies it at the Freud Museum London - I stumbled across a link to an exhibition at Slought, a non-profit organization on the campus of the University of Pennsylvania entitled... wait for it... 'Solitary Pleasures'! The organization's link is here and must be name-checked: https://slought.org/resources/solitary_pleasures

Mann & Frau & Animal

VALIE EXPORT

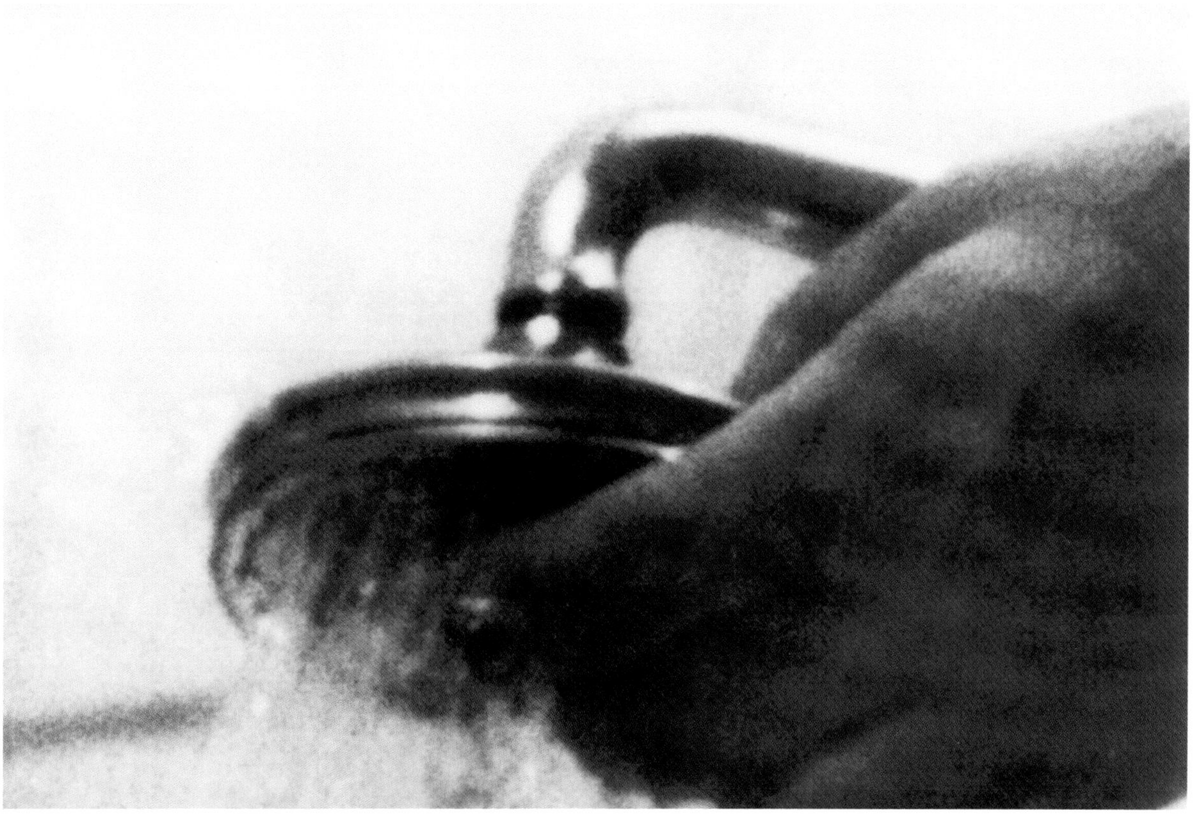

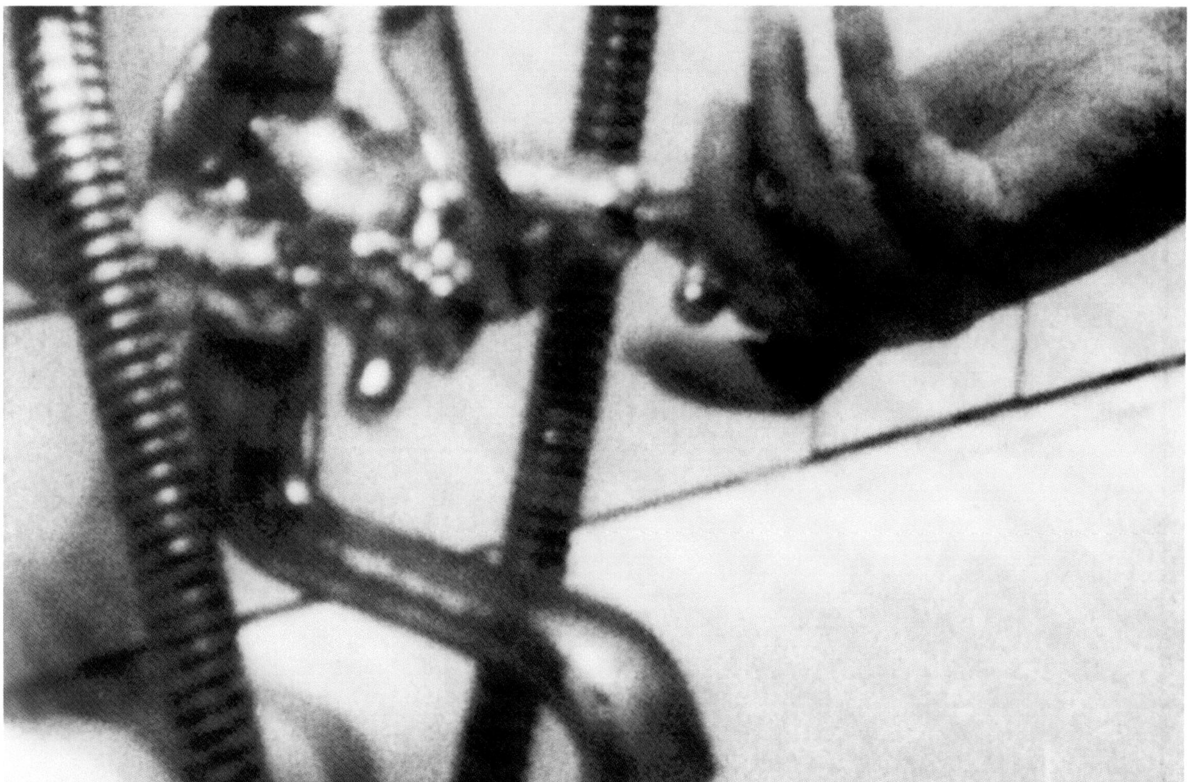

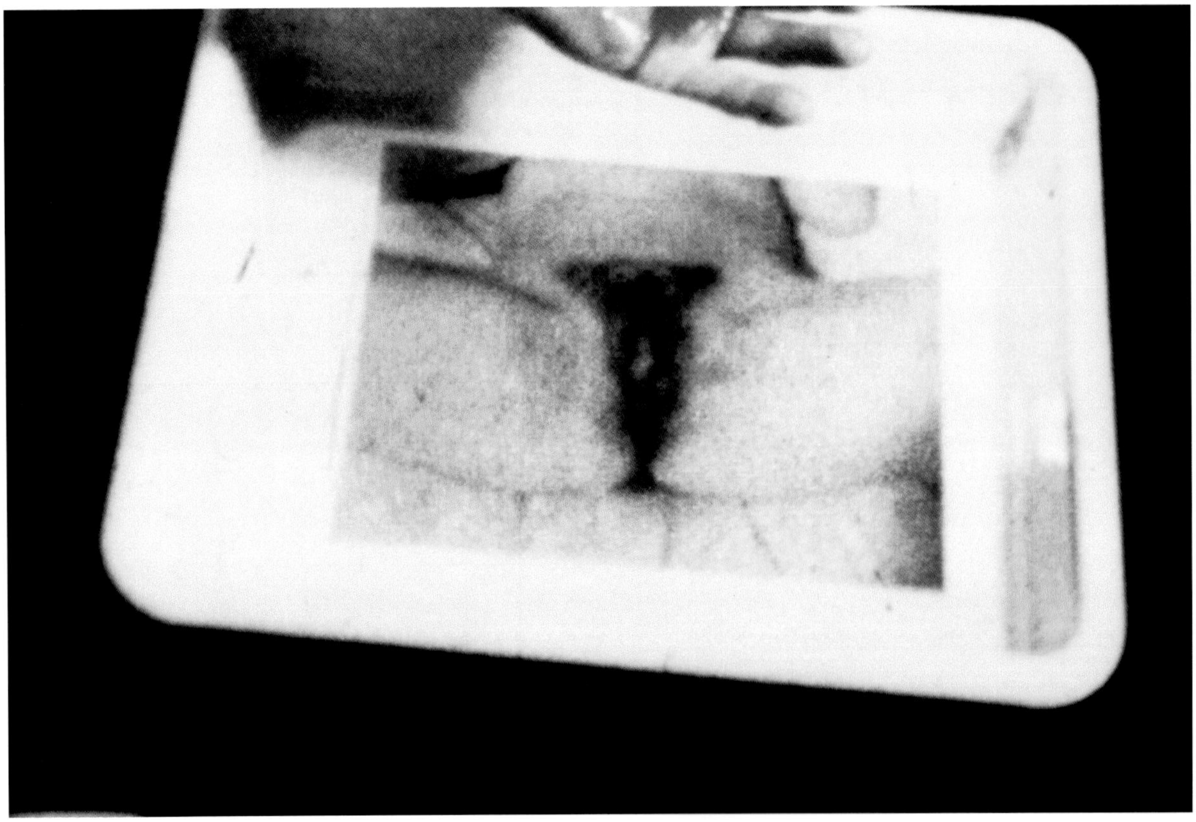

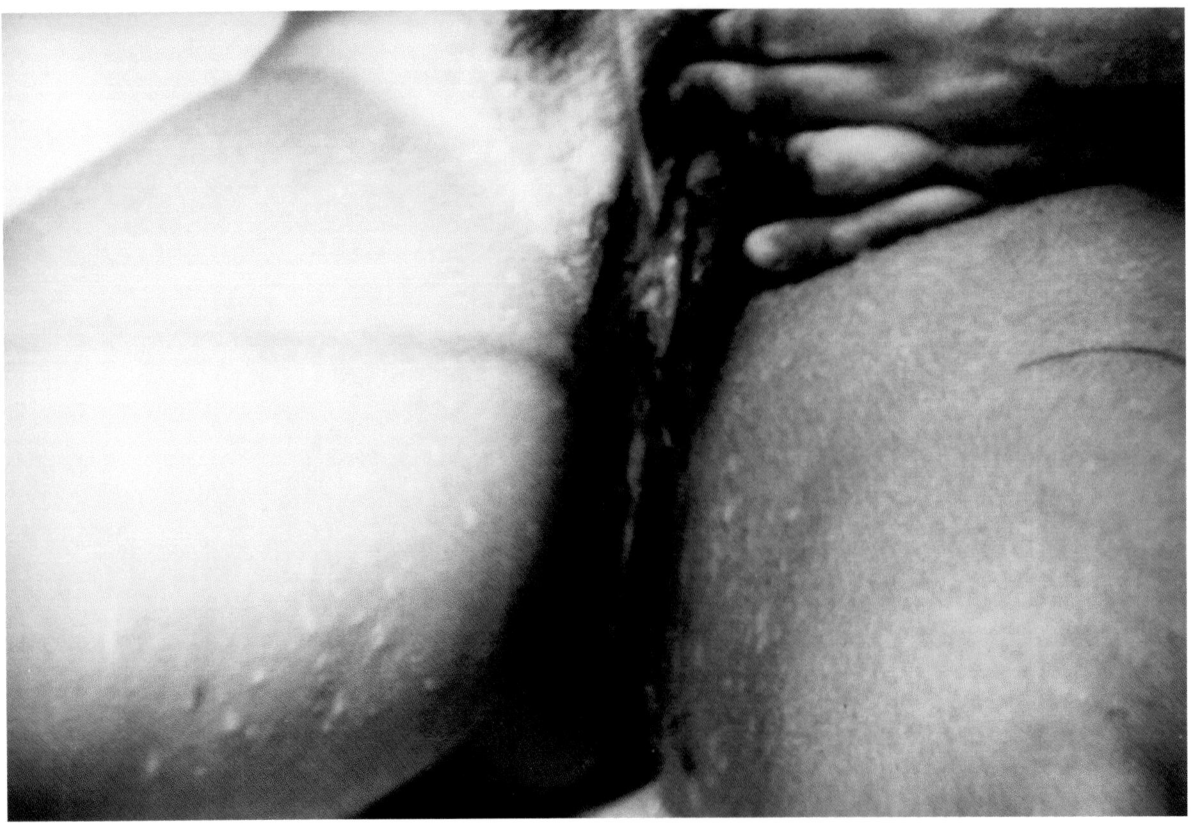

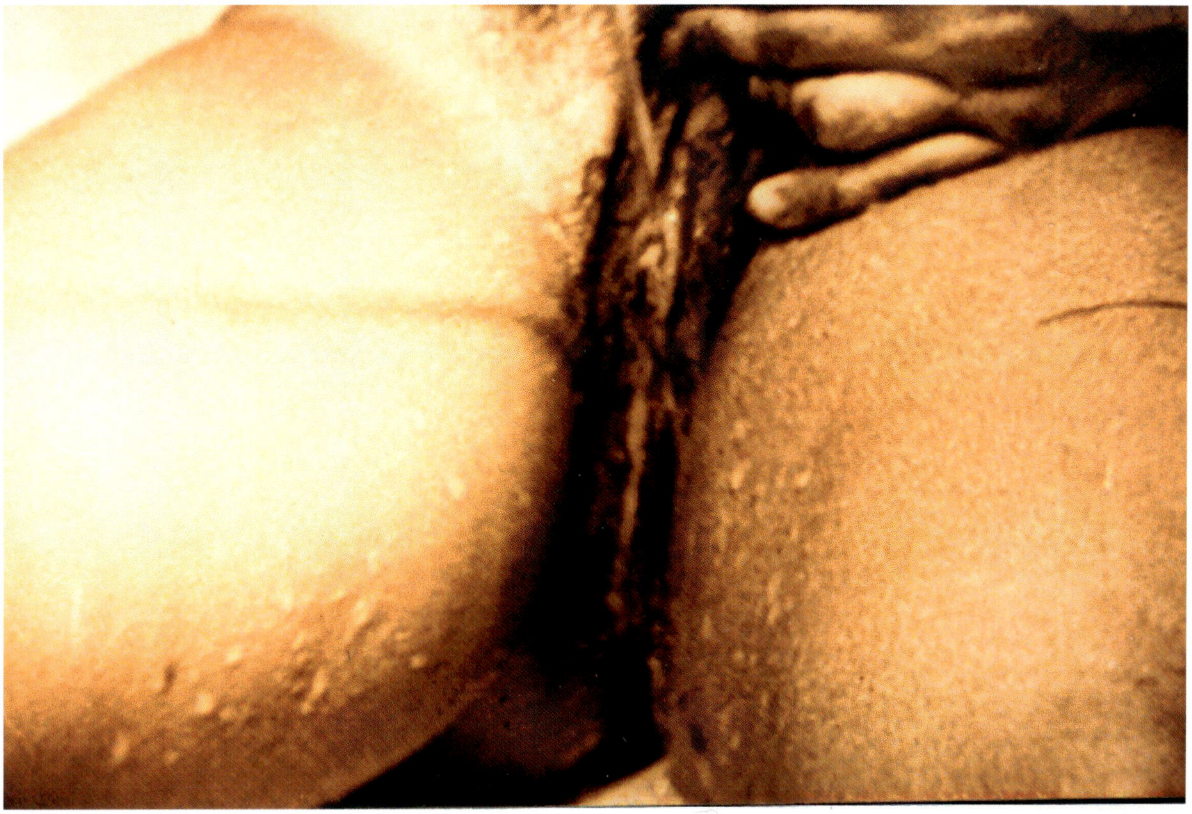

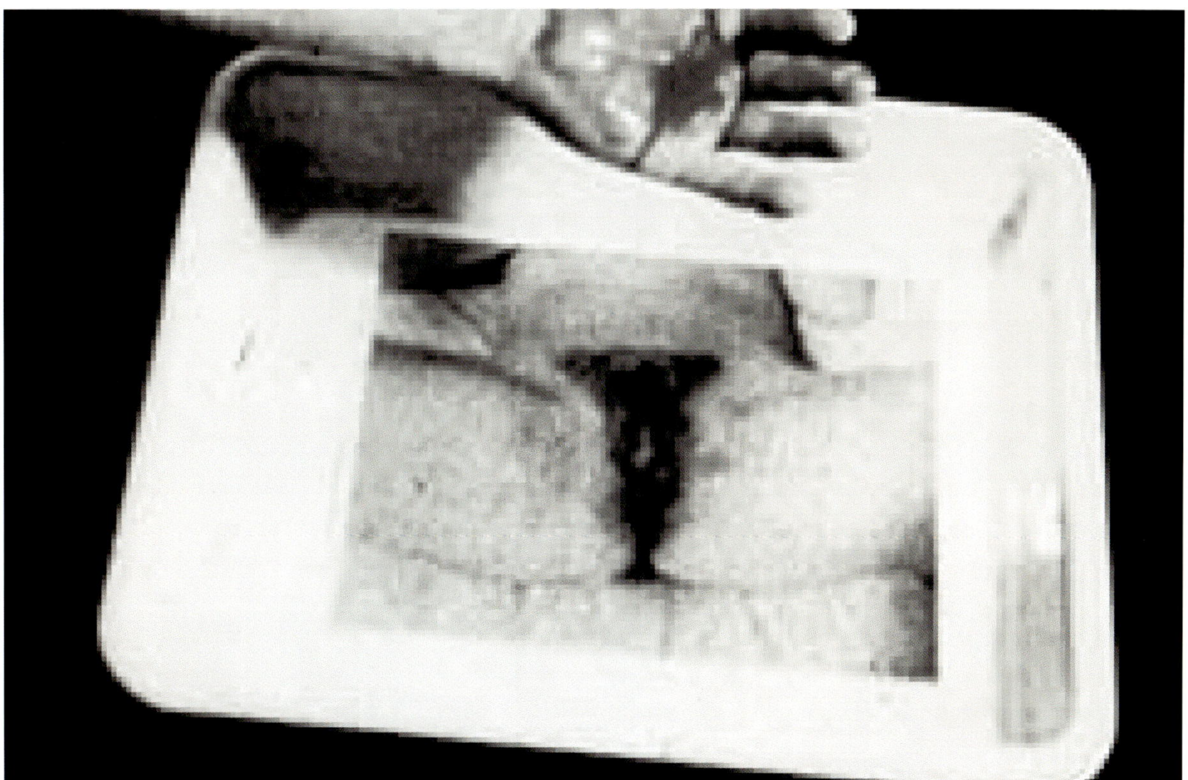

Regarding Masturbation

Thomas W. Laqueur

I want to respond in this short essay to a question posed to me by the editor of this publication and exhibition curator Marquard Smith: 'How has (and what does it mean that) masturbation', he asks 'has come to be regarded not only as a "substitution" for "proper" relations between human beings, sexuality and intimacy but perhaps even "a model for actual sex".'

'Regarded.' Throughout most of the long history of thinking about sex masturbation was not regarded at all: it was not something worth thinking about. Nameless until it took on Onan's name in the early eighteenth century - before then pretty much no-one thought that God had struck down Tamar's husband for his eponymous sin - it is hard to know whether someone was talking about our subject at all. Quips and pictures offer some clues that suggest that masturbation was a 'substitute' for proper sexual relations but only for those men for whom a sense of the proper scarcely mattered.(1)

Satyrs are shown masturbating on Greek krators, not so much as a substitute for something else but because they were insatiable and incapable of sexual decorum. Likewise in classical antiquity slaves and bumpkins and those too poor to afford alternatives. 'You have at your disposal a train of slaves,' bemoans the masturbator in satire by the Roman author Martial; 'I have to masturbate.' Literally, 'my hand comes to my assistance in lieu of Gannymede'. Remarks about women masturbating are rare before the eighteenth century; in Greece or Rome when it is remarked upon it is almost invariably about their using dildos when no penis was available. There is no female equivalent of the slave in Aristophanes' *Peace* who lazes about all afternoon masturbating, the ancestor of the modern wanker who fits into neither the substitution nor model category but into a third one about which more in a moment.

For almost two thousand years, that is until about 1712, there is little more to be said about our subject. Millennia's worth of brilliant Christian casuistry scarcely distinguish masturbation from a list of non-reproductive ways of having sex: women on top (supposedly not good for making babies), anal sex, coitus interruptus, and such.

'Regarded.' I should make clear the limits of Marquard Smith's question and my answer. We are talking here not about what people actually do or why they do it. There is very little evidence, historical or contemporary, on these matters. For example, Matt Young, a Iraq War veteran writes in his recent memoir *Eat the Apple* (Marine slang for 'Fuck the Corps') that masturbation is a means of survival. 'Jerking off has saved countless lives through countless wars,' presumably by mitigating the endless boredom and keeping soldiers awake on guard duty. If this were the case it would be neither a substitution for the real thing or a model for something else. Hard to say what it is. And has this always been so? Did Roman legionnaires jerk off along Hadrian's Wall or the Syrian frontier to keep awake? Young also has a whole chapter on inventive masturbatory techniques that argues for a substitution effect: rubber gloves and a towel as a sort of prosthetic vagina, a sort of military version of the civilian Portnoy's use of raw liver. What little ethnography we have will not take us very far in answering the question at hand.

Masturbation as we moderns have come to regard it is creature of the Enlightenment. It entered the world around 1712 in an obscure tract - *Onania* - by an anonymous author - whose definition of sex with oneself was wildly influential. Those who practice it 'whilst yielding to filthy imagination,' he wrote, 'endeavor to imitate and procure for themselves that sensation, which God ordained to attended to Carnal commerce of the two sexes.' There is in this description the claim of illicit substitution, self-pleasuring in place of the usual carnal commerce. And the author suggests why: girls can use it to 'combat strong desires,' and refuse bad matches; boys 'too bashful to approach girls' can get satisfaction anyway.

But the key words in *Onania*'s definition, ones which quickly made their way into thinking of the high Enlightenment's great figures - Kant, Rousseau, the authors of the *Encyclopédie* - fall largely outside our binaries of 'substitution' or 'model': 'imagination,' 'imitate,' 'procure for oneself'. It was less a question of substituting apples for oranges when citrus is unavailable - both real fruits enjoyed in the real world satisfying real bodily desires - so much as apples for fake apples eaten in solitude with no possibility of ever eating enough. Moderate masturbation as a way of satisfying normal sociable sexual desire - a substitution of one for the other - would not be so bad the *Encyclopédie* argued fifty years after *Onania*. But this is not the case. It was instead driven from within by a 'voluptuous, fiery imagination,' that had no connection with reality. Masturbating was not so much substituting one thing for another in the real world but a wallowing in a solitary world of the self.

Rousseau, the great prophet of solitude, was also one of the great Enlightenment critics of solitary sex. The masturbator - he is speaking of the eponymous Emile - is not so much substituting an affair with himself for an affair with an inappropriate woman - one kind of sex for another. If that were the case it would not be a problem; it could be stopped. Rather he is substituting the real world for a wholly interior one, real sex for the 'dangerous supplement' which nothing can satisfy because the engine of desire is wholly inside. In the real world there are limits: there is only so much 'real sex' one can have because one or the other partner has reached his or her physical limits or refuses to go on. Not so with the solitary kind that goes on obsessively like an engine without a governor. Solitary sex had become in the Enlightenment not so much a substitute - although that too - for real sex as the domain for a wholly different universe of sex: a sex of the imagination, a sex of the self in its own world.

By the twentieth century this view would become the basis for something new, for the alternative Marquard Smith suggests: 'a model for actual sex'. Let me more precise. It would become 'a model for solitary sex that is at the same time an act of self-fashioning in the real world just as are the various forms of "real", that is "social sex".' Freud was critical for this move.

He was in many ways old fashioned in his views of masturbation. Unlike most of his colleagues he thought, for example, that its obsessive quality, identified by Enlightenment thinkers, could cause actual physical harm. Few doctors held to that view by the early twentieth century. But he was revolutionary in regarding masturbation as characteristic of a stage in psychogenesis. He thought it crucial in the development of genital sexuality but that once that had been achieved it would be superseded by mature sex, that is heterosexual intercourse. This supersession was notoriously tricky for women who had to give up the primary site of genital pleasure, discovered through masturbation - the clitoris - for an altogether less propitious organ, from a neurological perspective - the vagina.

The normative precepts of Freud's story are less exigent today than its underlying premise that masturbation - solitary sex - is a way of becoming who one is - of self fashioning - that can at the same time be the basis of social sex. Masturbation has become 'actual sex' both because its place in the world has changed and because 'actual sex' has changed. It has come to be largely unanchored from its time immemorial mooring to reproduction. 'Actual sex' - at least in the prosperous western world - has, in its many and wild forms, thus been set free to do what masturbation had been condemned for in the eighteenth century. The two meet as zones of the imagination, of play, of imitation, of solitude that can easily morph into many forms of sociability.

Regarded: If I were to suggest a moment when Freud's insights became the basis for 'perhaps even a model for actual sex' it would be the very public feminist re-appropriation of the clitoris in the 1960's and 1970's that continues to the present. (There are of course other pivotal moments each with their own and overlapping histories: queerness, SM, bi, for starters.) There was an element of the substitution, without the mocking jokes of antiquity, in much of this. 'A woman needs a man like a fish needs a bicycle,' is not a claim about second best. But the more important aspect of much of the feminist writing on masturbation is that it is 'actual sex' in that it is actually about self discovery, that it is a form of proper relations with oneself which is in any case the first step to "proper" relations between human beings, sexuality and intimacy.'

Endnotes

1. The historical claims in this paragraph and in what follows are supported in Thomas W. Laqueur, *Solitary Sex: A Cultural History of Masturbation*, New York: Zone Books, 2003.

10 Haikus on Thumbsucking

Chantal Faust

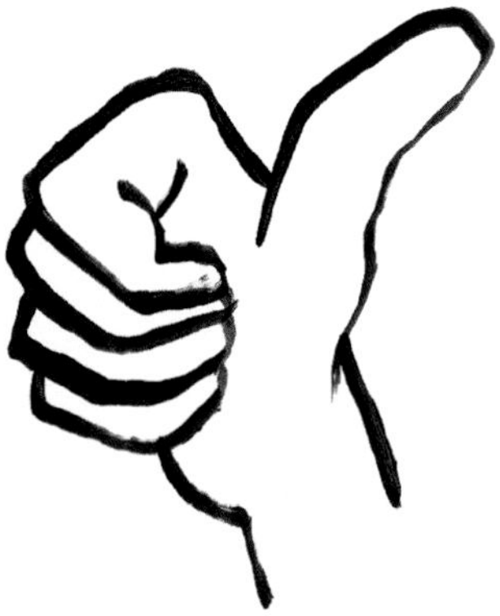

A simple action
With a complex construction
Behind it, repeats

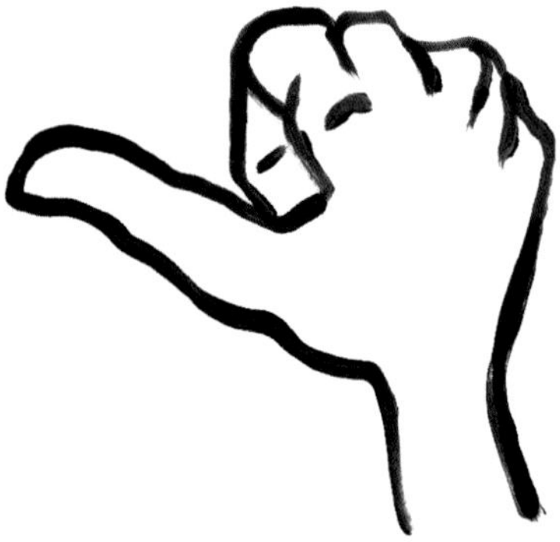

Why should it be such
Perfect a fit, if it was
Not meant to be there

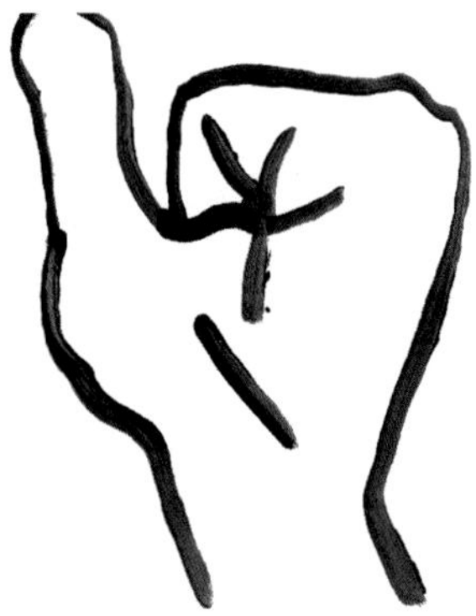

Is there another
Route beyond shame for the ones
Who dare continue

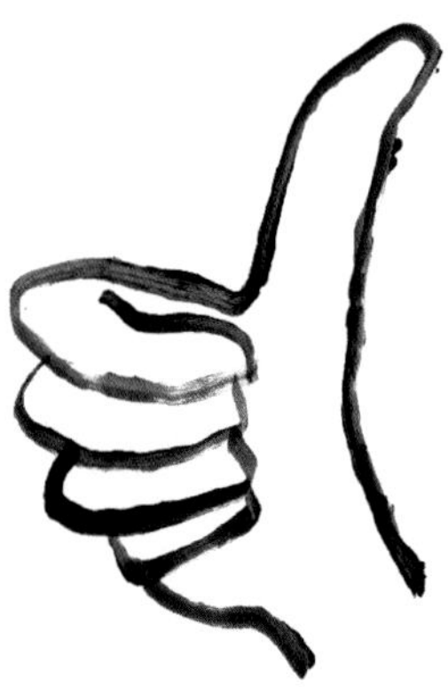

Will a thumb outlive
Its own body having spent
Life forever wet

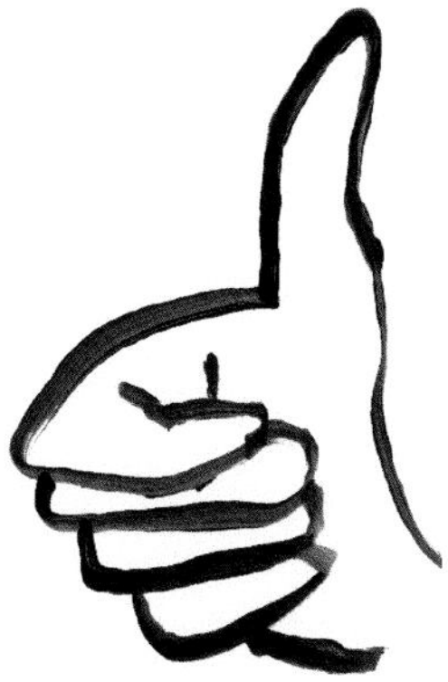

It's easy to point
Fingers at thumbs with little
Understanding of

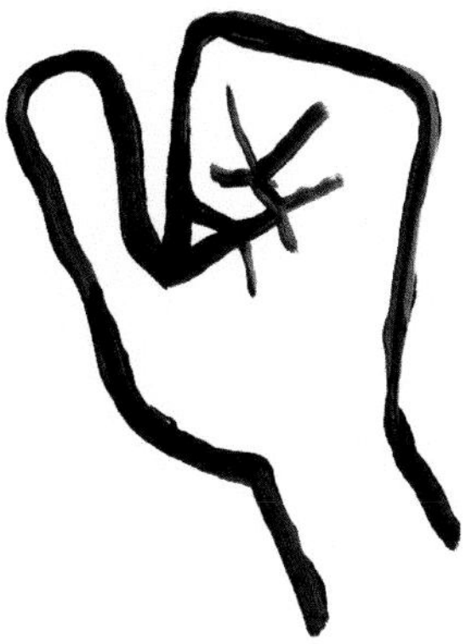

Perhaps it might be
Just about the sucking act
With no substitute

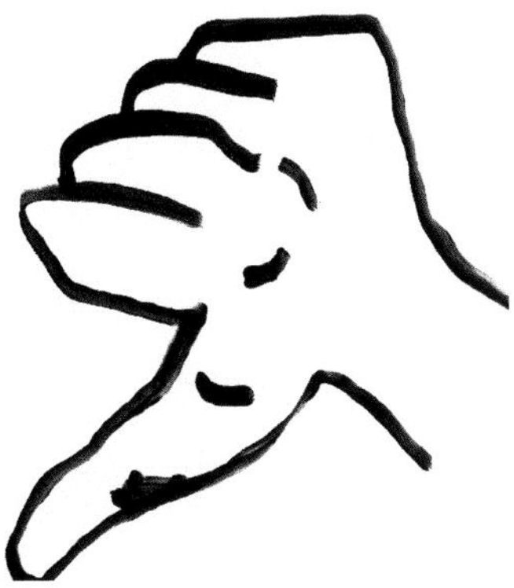

I can't understand
You with your thumb in your mouth
For the thousandth time

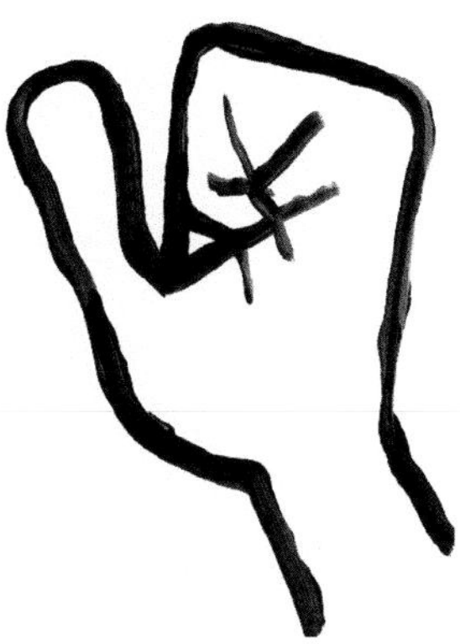

To suck rhythmically
And for no purpose except
To suck rhythmically

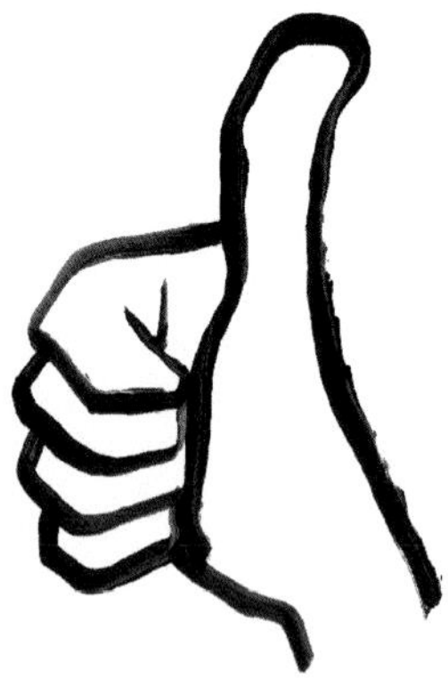

Short little moist stump
Knows just where it needs to be
On a bed of tongue

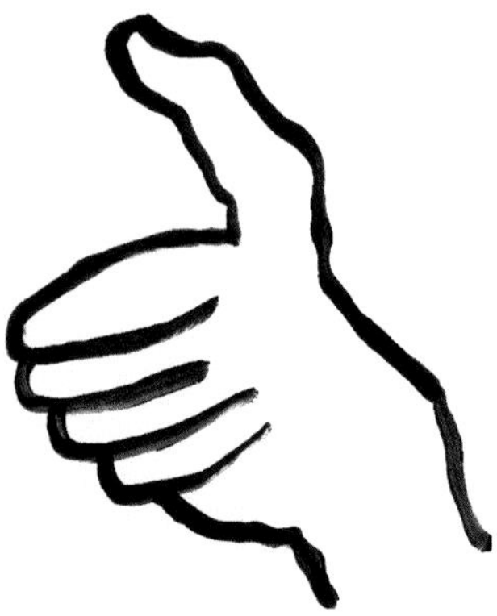

What happens to the
Sucking drive when denied and
Where does it go then?

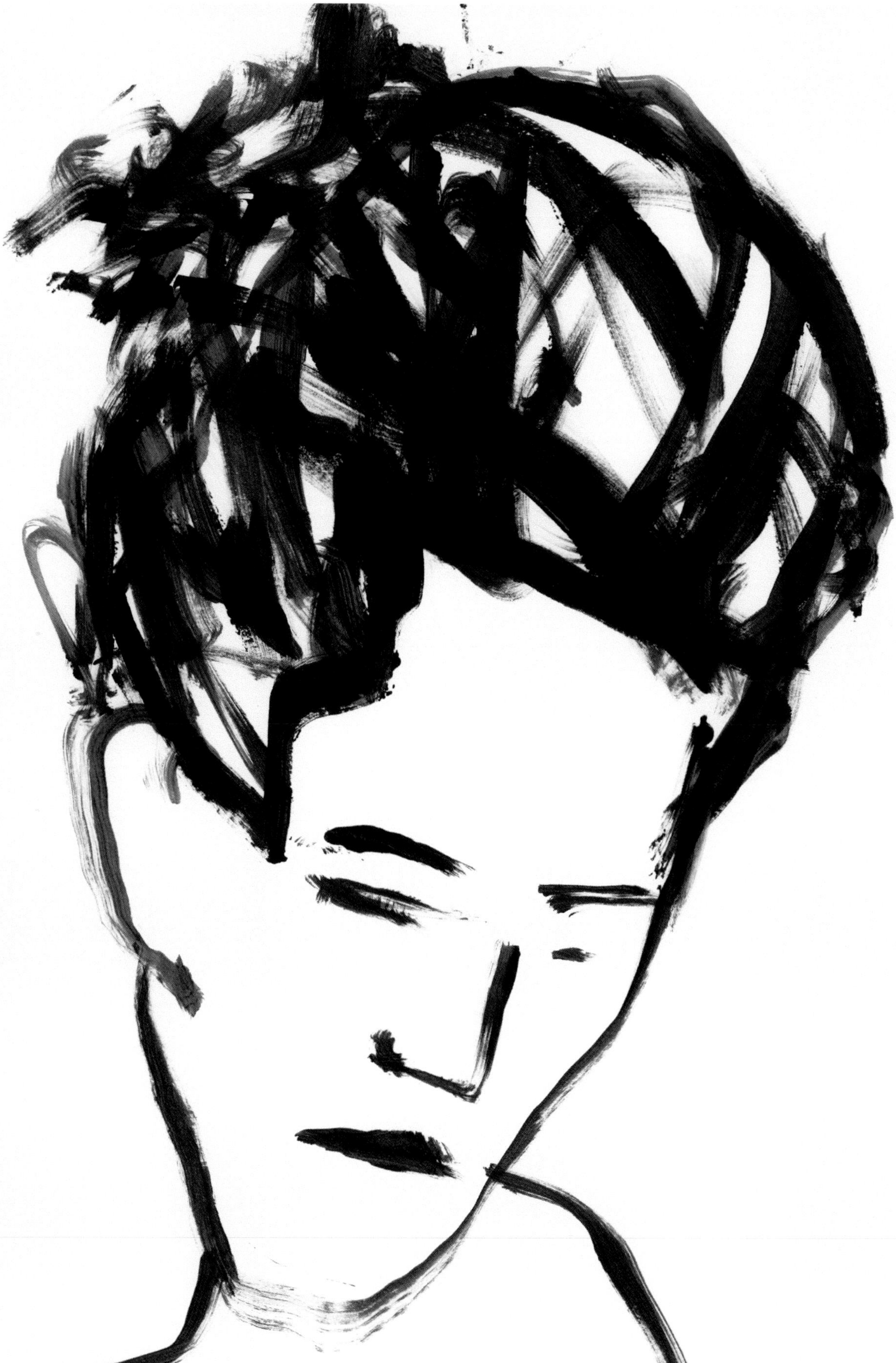

Making Glove or, Masturbation

Lee Edelman

In '"Civilized" Sexual Morality and the Modern Nervous Illness', Freud identifies some unfortunate consequences of the 'extreme measures' with which Western societies tend to restrict the 'sexual instinct.'(1) Among these he includes the 'by no means harmless' proclivity to masturbation that arises in response to social constraints on access to sexual intercourse. As his essay describes it, masturbation 'vitiates the character through *indulgence*' (CSM, 199), opening its practitioners to the horrors that from the eighteenth-century forward followed in masturbation's wake: otiosity, weakening of the vital energies, disengagement from external reality. Precisely insofar as it is always at hand, masturbation, Freud warns, 'teaches people to achieve important aims without taking trouble and by easy paths instead of through an energetic exertion of force' (CSM, 199). Even more threatening for a social order predicated on allo-erotic relations, it generates fantasies in which 'the sexual object is raised to a degree of excellence which is not easily found again in reality' (CSM, 200). Freud underlines this point by way of a witticism attributed to the Austrian writer, Karl Kraus: 'Copulation is no more than an unsatisfying substitute for masturbation' (CSM, 200).

In the lyrics to their comic song, 'Making Love Alone,' Marilyn Miller and Cheryl Hardwick enlarge on this perspective. As performed by Bernadette Peters in 1981 on *Saturday Night Live*, the song specifies the merits of 'the kind of love/ That fits hand in glove/ Especially when the glove is your own', calling particular attention to the certainty of pleasure that masturbation affords: 'there's a certain special magic/ To the touch of your own hand/ And a special thrill/ Knowing that you will/ For sure soon be feeling grand'. Unlike sexual intercourse, whose pathway to satisfaction passes through relations with another, masturbation collapses the distance between the agent of pleasure and its object. It provides release, to Freud's consternation, without the morally-instructive 'exertion of force' by forestalling the relational labor entailed in procuring an external object and circumventing the reality principle's limitations on hallucinatory pleasure.

But while auto-erotic experience, as Freud writes in 'Hysterical Phantasies and Their Relation to Bisexuality', begins as a simple 'procedure for the purpose of obtaining pleasure from some part of the body', it later 'merge[s] with a wishful idea from the sphere of object-love', that is to say, with a sexual phantasy, to which it then gets 'soldered'.(2) Freud places much weight on this soldering of bodily sensations to wishful ideas in order to affirm the inextricability of sexuality from the logic of phantasy and to interpret hysterical symptoms as 'unconscious phantasies brought into view' (HP, 162). By means of such somatizations, he writes, 'the giving up of the habit of masturbation is in fact undone' (CSM, 201). The inhibited aim of masturbation, which the hysteric had consciously renounced, returns through an 'approximation' of the 'original, primary sexual satisfaction' (HP, 162).

What this soldering costs us all, however, does not engage Freud's interest: the loss of auto-erotic pleasure *without* a mobilized phantasy. If the somatization of unconscious phantasy gives hysterics who have renounced masturbation the possibility of its 'sexual satisfaction', then the corollary is that masturbatory activity, absent the reinforcement of phantasy, may no longer achieve its aim. Masturbation's assured satisfaction, as presupposed by Freud and Kraus and as praised by Miller and Hardwick, thus conceals another prospect rarely acknowledged or discussed: masturbatory failure or blockage. As 'blockage' suggests, this condition can figure a condition particularly distressing for writers, artists, and other creators who use themselves as their own material in order to 'express themselves'. Indeed, the etymology of 'express' (from the Latin *ex* for 'out' and *pressare*, 'to press'), turns the very expression, 'to express oneself' into a figure for masturbation.

No artist has more vividly depicted the excruciating confluence of aesthetic and masturbatory failure than David Lynch in *Mulholland Drive*. When the character played by Naomi Watts - identified at this point in the movie as Diane, a would-be actress who relies on her lover, Camilla, for bit parts in films - discovers Camilla's involvement with Adam Kesher, Camilla's director, she finds herself utterly destitute: isolated, grieving her loss of Camilla, and filled with a bitter rage. Hoping to escape, at least for a moment, the reality that has swallowed her dreams, Diane, having literally shut the door on Camilla's offer of friendship, tries to assert her autonomy and self-sufficiency through masturbation. Lynch's camera pans from the now closed door to the couch on which it finds Diane, her breath coming heavily - half sob, half pant - as she tries to get herself off. After framing her face in close-up, the strain of her effort showing in her narrowed eyes and half-open mouth, Lynch cuts to a jerky, out-of-focus shot that refuses immediate legibility. As Diane's moans turn into a muted wail, though, the shot comes into focus, revealing itself as the point of view from her recumbent position on the couch gazing toward the decorative stones surrounding the fireplace directly across from it. The viewer may have been frustrated by the shot's illegibility, but when it resolves into definition it does so to indicate *Diane's* frustration. Try as she may to escape the maddening reality of her world, the stony vision literalizes her blocked access to pleasurable phantasy. Though the image will briefly lose focus again as she struggles to enter the dream-place of her hallucinatory fulfillment, the increasingly violent motion of her hand thrust deep into her pants is helpless to bring her the release or the sexual satisfaction she desires - helpless because she desires to desire from a place beyond desire, the place of a suicidal encounter with the body unenlivened by attachment to the world.

In this film whose power derives from its flooding of reality by phantasy, from its seductive insistence on the psychic interanimation of the two, this moment of desolate masturbation when the sustaining framework of phantasy fails and bodily pleasure proves impossible, seems almost like the navel of the dream as which *Mulholland Drive* takes shape. Visualizing in the stones of the fireplace, diegetically empty as they are, the absence of the 'wishful idea[s]' or phantasies to which pleasure finds itself 'soldered', the film offers a glimpse of the bedrock that reality rests on and conceals: the world without the expressive subject, untouched by its point of view. The perspective that takes in the stones, therefore, must be seen as the point of view of one unable to claim it as hers because she has lost all point in viewing. To reassert a point of view, to have a perspective from which to see, she would need to lose herself in phantasy and thereby attach to her body once more. Wallace Stevens, in 'Le Monocle de Mon Oncle', declared: 'If sex were all, then every trembling hand/ Could make us squeak, like dolls, the wished-for words'. But Freud and Lynch understand, to the contrary, that precisely insofar as sex *is* 'all', insofar as we take shape as subjects within the phantasy-relations it constructs, the hand alone will not suffice to make us squeak with pleasure. That hand, to return to the metaphor Miller and Hardwick make so much of, must always be gloved in phantasy.

Masturbation, then, is more for Lynch than a 'solitary pleasure'. Indeed, conceived as 'pleasure', masturbation is never solitary: it is 'soldered' to a structuring phantasy whose logic sustains us in the world. Through the generalization of this logic, to which auto-eroticism first succumbs, masturbation in the widest sense (in other words, as Freud himself puts it, 'not in its restricted literal sense of manual friction' [HP, 161]), keeps us from the destitution of encountering the obduracy of the Real, the persistence outside expression of something beyond the pleasure principle: the void of the subject stripped of its animation by desire. Masturbatory modes of 'getting off' thus work, paradoxically, to keep us *on* the path of relationality. Diane's unsuccessful masturbation speaks to the reduction that denies her relation at once to the world and to herself, making her the meaningless counterpart of the stones that she perceives, as if, like Stevens's 'Snow Man', she here encounters herself as 'nothing' and, unbearably, in the form of that nothing, 'beholds/ Nothing that is not there and the nothing that is'. Masturbatory phantasy defends against such self-annihilations, making the subject and its body come together, as fitted as hand and glove. In *Mulholland Drive,* though, Lynch takes the gloves off and shows that the hand is nothing without them.

Endnotes

1. Sigmund Freud, '"Civilized' Sexual Morality and Modern Nervous Illness', in *The Standard Edition of the Complete Psychological Works of Sigmund Freud,* (1959) Vol. 9, trans. and ed. James Strachey (London: Hogarth Press), p. 197. Subsequent page references to this work will be given in parentheses after the citation in the body of the text preceded by CSM.
2. Sigmund Freud, 'Hysterical Phantasies and Their Relation to Bisexuality', in *The Standard Edition of the Complete Psychological Works of Sigmund Freud*, (1959) Vol. 9, trans. and ed. James Strachey (London: Hogarth Press), p. 161. Subsequent page references to this work will be given in parentheses after the citation in the body of the text preceded by HP.

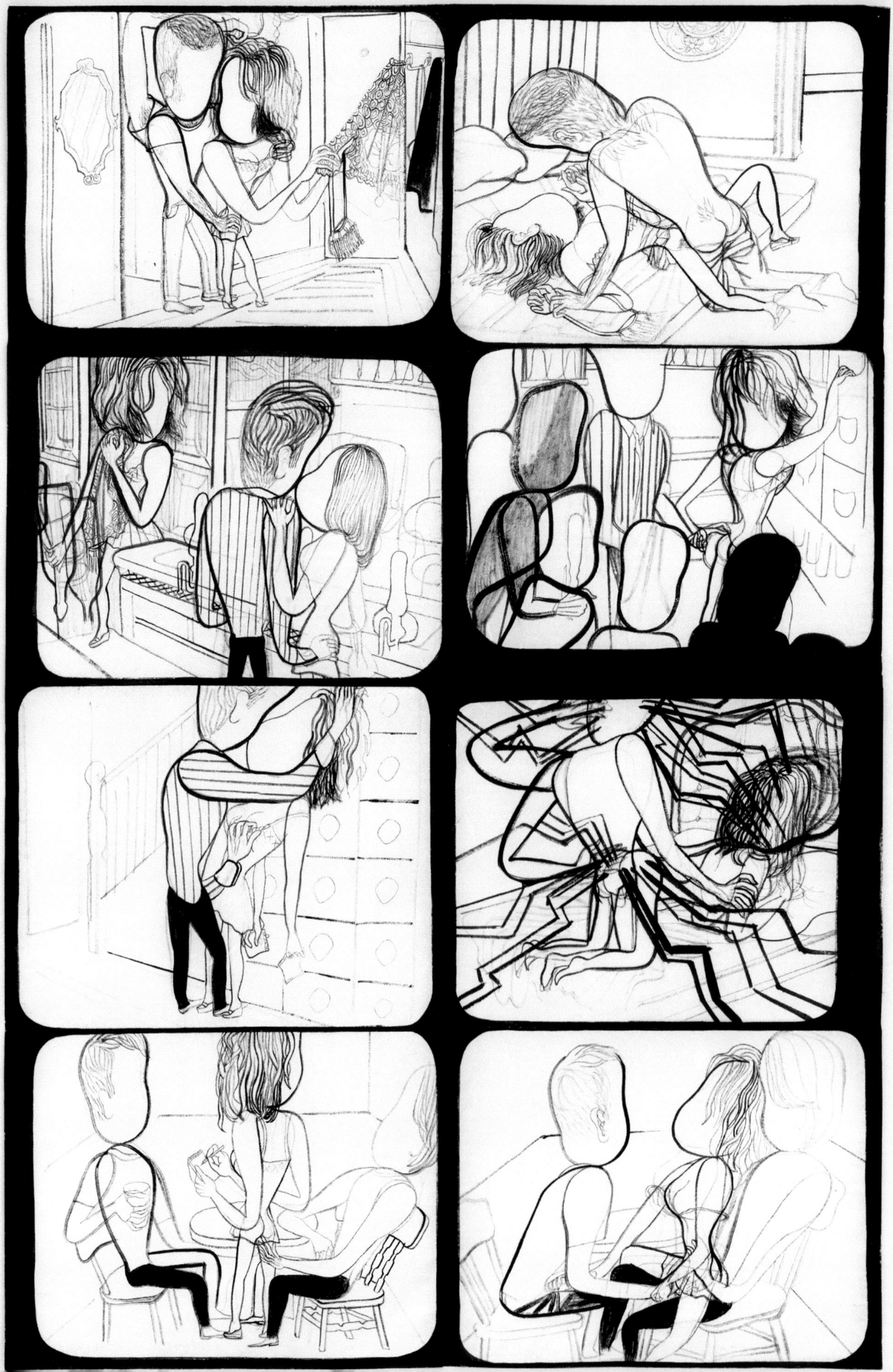

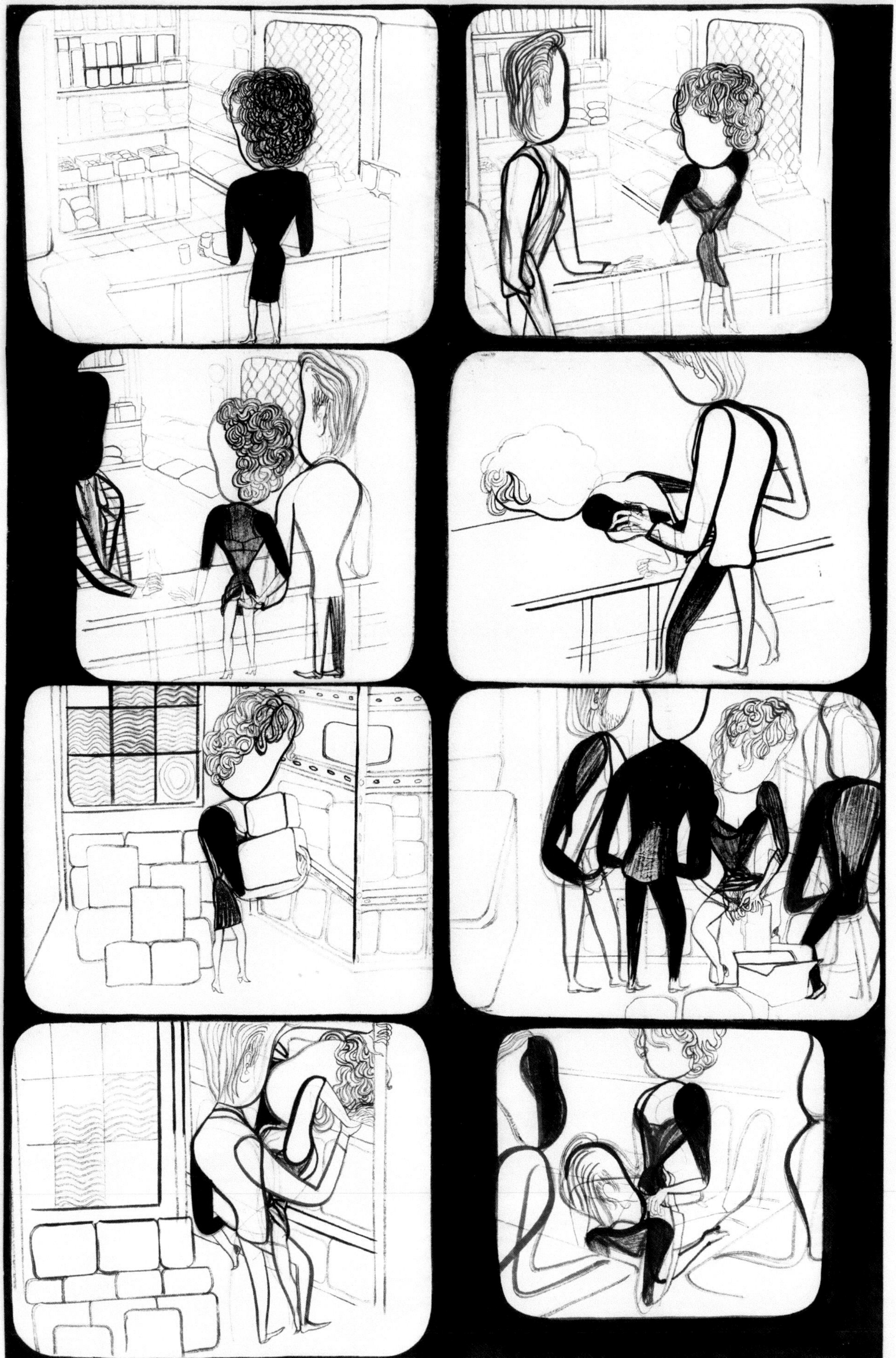

Whacking and Strumming: A Freudian View

Ivan Ward

When students first encounter Freud they say he is 'weird'. If pressed to explain themselves, perhaps during a visit to the Freud Museum, they may even suggest that he is 'a bit of a pervert'; a loner and a loser, locking himself away in his room while thinking about sex. What they imagine he is doing in his room is an activity that I daresay some of the teenage students engage in themselves – but it is one tainted with shame and embarrassment and the spectre of 'perversion'. As if to confirm that the shameful part of the activity is what's going on in your head, the taint of masturbation may attach itself to thinking in general, and the phrase 'intellectual wanker' adequately summarises this attitude. Who wants to be one of those?

Freud would have understood the students' concern and perhaps agreed with much of it. His attitude to masturbation was curiously old-fashioned, and he related the damaging effects of masturbation to its capacity to turn you away from 'real life'. My experience writing this paper is a case in point. Only now, with the deadline upon me, am I forcing myself to write something, and it is a struggle. Prior to that I have been enjoying myself immensely, with a bucketful of great ideas, and pleasuring myself in a fantasy world that had no need to engage with the reality of organising thoughts, finding words to communicate them, testing arguments or looking for evidence. In masturbation, whether of the physical or intellectual variety, 'the libido turns away from reality' says Freud, and 'is taken over by imaginative activity'. As a sexual act there is also a danger on the level of sexuality itself: it 'strengthens the images of the first sexual objects and becomes fixated to them' (Freud 1912, p. 182).

That is Freud's main concern. If you get stuck in a masturbatory life-style you end up mired in your childhood family psychodrama and don't engage in the struggle to find a real 'sexual object'. Of course the conscious masturbation fantasies soon find substitutes for the incestuous figures, but the latter remain active in the unconscious. 'In this way it can happen that the whole of a young man's sensuality becomes tied to incestuous objects in the unconscious, or to put it another way, becomes fixated to unconscious incestuous phantasies.' And the consequences of this masturbatory activity can be more-than-serious. 'The result is then total impotence, which is perhaps further ensured by the simultaneous onset of an actual weakening of the organs that perform the sexual act' (Freud 1912, p. 182). One almost expects Freud to add: 'And it makes you go blind'!

Yet in the furtive and secretive aspects of masturbation that both Freud and the students acknowledge, they show that it is difficult to think of the activity as an unalloyed 'pleasure'; while, given its fantasy element, filled with mental pictures of other people and stimulating erotic scenarios, can we really say it is 'solitary'? Steve Dwoskin's thoughtful and courageous independent film *Moment* (1969), in which a static camera records a woman's face while she is masturbating to orgasm, eschews pornographic conventions in an attempt to circumvent the violence of the voyeuristic gaze. Despite acknowledging the presence of the camera, she seems to be in a world of her own, yet the fiction is undermined by the simple fact that we are watching a film and a moment that has passed. On screen itself, the cigarette that the protagonist is smoking points to a world of fantasy beyond the diegetic moment and marks an inevitable fault line in the autoerotic encounter. Whether we see it or not, more than one person is involved; the self is divided between active and passive, male and female, giving and receiving, which even without the presence of a camera might lead us to suspect the function of an 'other' within the ritualised process. Taking it as a 'sexual act' we might have to agree with Freud when he wrote: 'I am accustoming myself to regarding every sexual act as a process in which four individuals are involved' (Freud, 1899).

If 'solitary' is dubious, 'pleasure' is equally so. Psychoanalysts are notoriously pessimistic when it comes to the possibility of 'pleasure' since how can you get one unambiguous result from a theory based on the idea of psychic conflict? There is always a countercurrent, always a worm in the bud. Freud led the way by arguing for a quasi-biological obstacle to the achievement of pleasure in the sexual arena, perhaps the most radical statement ever made about the subject:

> It is my belief that, however strange it may sound, we must reckon with the possibility that something in the nature of the sexual instinct itself is unfavourable to the realization of complete satisfaction (Freud, 1912, pp. 188-9).

But if it is not pleasure as such that masturbation aims for, perhaps it is 'beyond pleasure'. The factor of repetition and the rhythmic nature of the activity itself indicates that masturbation might fruitfully be related to the 'repetition compulsion', and indeed Freud hinted as much:

> It has dawned on me that masturbation is the one major habit, the 'primal addiction' he writes to his friend Wilhelm Fliess, 'and that it is only as a substitute and replacement for it that the other addictions – for alcohol, morphine, tobacco, etc. - come into existence (Freud, 1897).

Of course he includes his own 'solitary vice' of smoking on the list, even if it was not always solitary, but it is notable that all these 'substitutes' are self-destructive activities that might even be described as 'self-abuse'. Thirty years later, Freud had not changed his mind. In his paper on Dostoevsky he adds gambling to the list of substitutes, citing as evidence that 'the emphasis laid upon the passionate activity of the hands betrays this derivation' (Freud, 1928, p. 193).

When students wonder what Freud is doing alone in his room - imagining it has some sexual connotation and something to do with his hands - I sometimes remind them what they might be doing in their own rooms, playing video games or texting to their friends. In the same paper on Dostoevsky Freud broadens the scope of the argument in a surprising way.

> Indeed, the passion for play is an equivalent of the old compulsion to masturbate; 'playing' is the actual word used in the nursery to describe the activity of the hands upon the genitals (ibid. p. 193).

Perhaps this is the passage Winnicott is remembering when he vehemently objects to the psychoanalytic equation of 'play' and 'masturbation'. (Winnicott, 1971, p. 39) And he is right to do so. Play is not masturbation - but Freud does not say it is. Rather, certain forms of play may be substitutes for masturbation when the child realises that 'playing with himself' is disapproved of and he starts to buckle under the weight of 'sexual intimidation' (Freud, 1924, p. 179).

It is a small step from 'substitute' to 'sublimation'. By adding 'play' to the litany of dangerous addictions we could look instead at the positive sublimations that might be derived from masturbation and its vicissitudes. Although it does not entirely disappear during the period of latency, the earlier masturbatory activity is now clothed with furtive shame and becomes a site of unequal struggle for the growing child. On learning that Princess Diana's butler was apparently dispatched to the newsagents to procure 'wank mags' for her sons, novelist Howard Jacobson regretted what the boys were missing by having the butler do the shopping. 'No listening to the libido as it shapes its promptings, no mustering of the forces of resistance, no argument between the Jekyll and the Hyde of one's sexual nature, which argument Jekyll will always lose, but only after the libido has flooded the whole system with those chemicals to which we give the simple name of desire, but which in fact also encompasses self-loathing and self-destruction and insanity' (Jacobson, 2002). Could it be that the centuries old war on masturbation, and the puzzling sense of 'sin' attached to it, is not a simple conspiracy of church or state, but an index of a danger at the heart of sexual expression itself?

Freud puts it like this:

> When the (male) child's interest turns to his genitals he betrays the fact by manipulating them frequently; and he then finds that the adults do not approve of this behaviour. More or less plainly, more or less brutally, a threat is pronounced that this part of him which he values so highly will be taken away from him (Freud, 1924 p. 174).

The child's 'phallic genital organisation', as Freud calls it, which began so promisingly with the cocksure exhibitionism of the pre-Oedipal child, is gradually destroyed by the threat of castration. 'Not immediately, it is true, and not without other influences being brought to bear as well' (Freud, 1924, p. 175).

So what happens to all that manic energy? What happens to the tidal wave of emotion that has been unleashed during the Oedipal maelstrom?

> The libidinal trends belonging to the Oedipus complex are in part desexualized and sublimated... and in part inhibited in their aim and changed into impulses of affection. The whole process has, on the one hand, preserved the genital organ - has averted the danger of its loss - and, on the other, has paralysed it - has removed its function. This process ushers in the latency period, which now interrupts the child's sexual development (Freud, 1924 p. 177).

You go to school. Learn to read. You find something to do that binds the energy, modulates the inchoate urges and fantasies, attenuates the anxiety. Something repetitive is good, something that occupies the hands or inhibits their function. In my day, boys spent hours kicking a ball from foot to foot to keep it from touching the ground while girls played cat's cradle or French skipping or two balls against the wall, with increasingly elaborate repetitive patterns.

Cricket genius Don Bradman found such an activity in his youth. He would spend countless hours of solitary practice hitting a ball against the garden wall of his Adelaide home, making the task more difficult for himself by hitting a *golf ball* with a *cricket stump*. The Don didn't just whack the ball with a stick, he hit it in a highly controlled and 'inhibited' way, with the factor of repetition as predominant. Bradman's repetitive ritual, like my own and countless others at the same age, was a substitute for masturbation. Or rather, it was a 'compromise formation'. It is a surrogate masturbation activity, but it also embodies the prohibition against masturbation; it expresses aggression and it controls aggression; it enacts a fantasy of triumph and 'transcendence', with the exhilaration and joy of passing each milestone of ritual achievement, while it expresses submission to reality as represented by 'the laws of nature'. In engaging in a socially acceptable activity the child controls both the inner world of dangerous temptation and the outer world of paternal disapproval. As Freud might put it, the libidinal currents are 'tamed' and diverted in their course. Embodied in these simple repetitive acts are the sublimated fears and desires of a latency-aged child. And even if we cannot predict their final outcome, in their unconscious meaning lies the deep well of emotion from which can spring future greatness. In contrast to the agitated ritual of his youth, Bradman's mature batting technique was characterised by an almost Buddha-like stillness when facing the bowler.

In another field altogether, comedian Billy Connolly found a calming influence in his troubled young life when he took up playing the banjo. 'Something about the playing of this instrument, perhaps the regular strumming and repetition of phrases, was surprisingly soothing for him' suggests his wife and biographer Pamela Stephenson, 'From then on, he and his banjo could barely be prised apart' (Stephenson 2002, p136). In their daily life together she is not so enamoured. Recounting a typical family argument the symbolic meaning of the instrument and the anxiety it evades is not far from the surface.

> What's the difference between a banjo and an onion? I tease him. 'Nobody cries when you slice up a banjo'.
>
> 'How many banjo players does it take to change a lightbulb?' he returns. "Just one, but he does it over and over again..." (Stephenson, p. 140)

It is probably no surprise to discover that in one of his legendary stage performances, Connolly treats his audience to a graphic masterclass in advanced masturbation.

'The opening line is all-important', explains Billy. 'Say "Thank God you're here!"'(Stephenson, p. 56).

If the impact of the castration complex marks a hiatus between the early flowering of childhood masturbation and its later manifestation as a guilty secret, as I am suggesting, then it also marks a moment of new creative possibilities. Perhaps this is a time to reconsider the developmental function of masturbation - from substitute for addiction to creative sublimation.

Bibliography

Dwoskin, Steve (1969) *Moment*, 12 minute film featuring Tina Fraser. BFI online at https://player.bfi.org.uk/free/film/watch-moment-1969-online

Freud, S (1897) Letter from Freud to Fliess, December 22, *The Complete Letters of Sigmund Freud to Wilhelm Fliess, 1887-1904,* (1985) edited by Jeffrey Moussaieff Masson. Cambridge, Mass: Belknap Press of Harvard University Press.

Freud, S. (1899) Letter from Freud to Fliess, August 1, 1899.

Freud, S (1912) 'On the universal tendency to debasement in the sphere of love', *Standard Edition of the Complete Psychological Works of Sigmund Freud*, edited by James Strachey, Vol XI. London: Hogarth.

Freud, S (1924) 'The Dissolution of Oedipus Complex', SE Vol. XIX.

Freud, S (1928) 'Dostoevsky and Parricide', SE Vol. XXI.

Jacobson, Howard (2002) 'It's the furtive shame that makes a boy a man,' *The Independent* Saturday 9 November.

Stephenson, Pamela (2002) *Billy,* London: Harper Collins.

Winnicott, D.W. (1971) *Playing and Reality,* London: Tavistock Publications.

THE FRUIT IS THERE TO BE EATEN

Written by

Michelle Williams Gamaker

SHOOTING SCRIPT 1B
18 July 2016

michellewilliamsgamaker.com

KANCHI

5 cont.

How many of us will <u>actually</u> travel, and which immigration border will test our botanical knowledge?

Kanchi looks back out the window. Points at the mountain. She STANDS UP and begins to recite her own alphabet. An invocation for the oppressed.

KANCHI (CONT'D)

Ann is African.
Bill is bisexual..
Caroline is a cartographer.
David is from Darjeeling.
Edward is in Egypt.
Freddy is female.
Grace is a guy.
Henry speaks Hindi.
Ian is Intersex.
John is jaded.
Kitty loves kwaito.
Lucy loves Lucy.
Mary is a masochist.
Nancy knows Nehru.
Oliver is open.
Peter is Pan.
Queenie is questioning.
Robert has rabies.
Simon is Sinhalese.
Tommy is Tamil.
Ursula is undecided.
Vera visits Venus.
William is worldly.
Xena dabbles in xenomancy.
Yolanda says yes.
Zachary is a zealot.

SISTER CLODAGH

How can you be so sure that you are not travelling already?

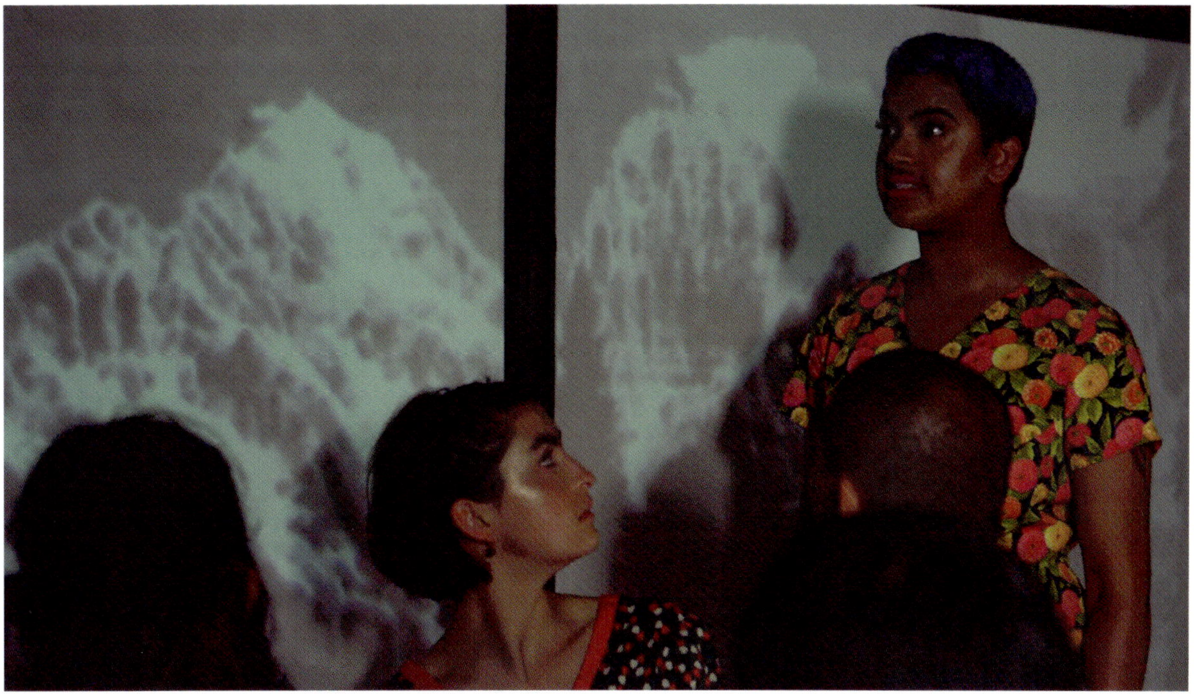

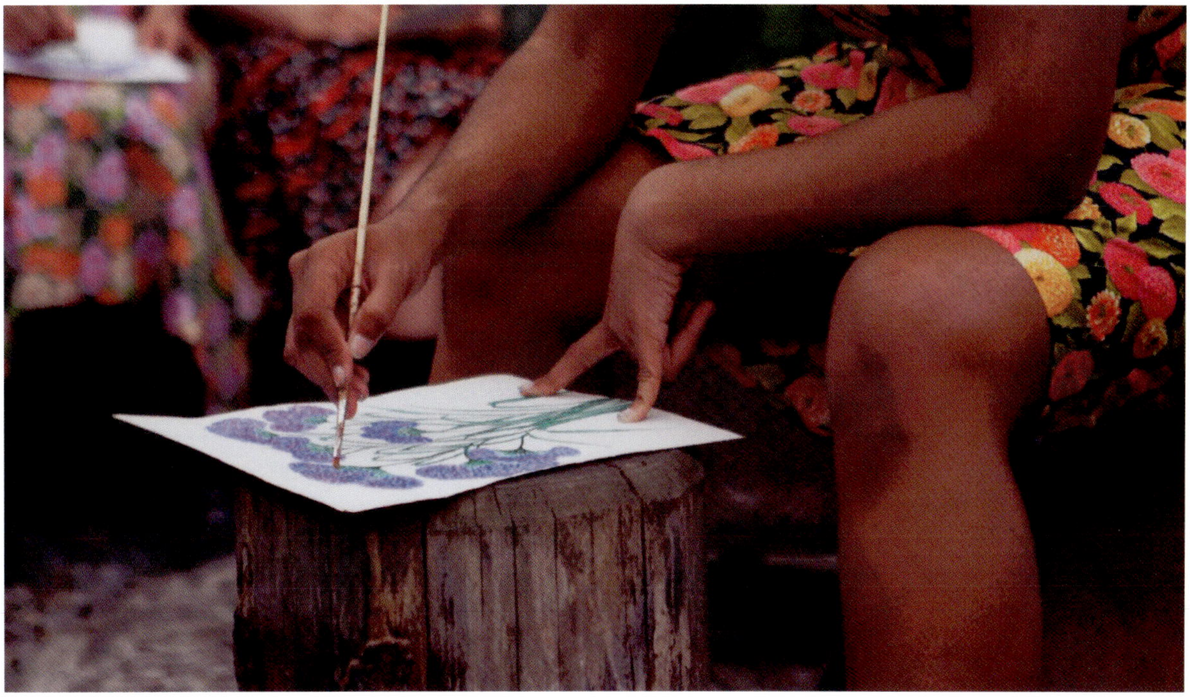

Kanchi smirks. She replies by rolling up her sleeve to reveal A TATTOO OF A FLOWER yet to be named.

Sister Clodagh approaches her and inspects the artwork, trying to make sense of its symbolism.

INT. DORMITORY - NIGHT 6

SISTER PHILIPPA, 50s, overweight, kneels beside her BED, praying. She is preparing for bed.

TAROT CARDS are scattered on the floor.

She opens her eyes.

She turns and has an ecstatic vision of FLOWERS in bloom on her bedroom wall.

The moment enthralls and terrifies her in equal measure.

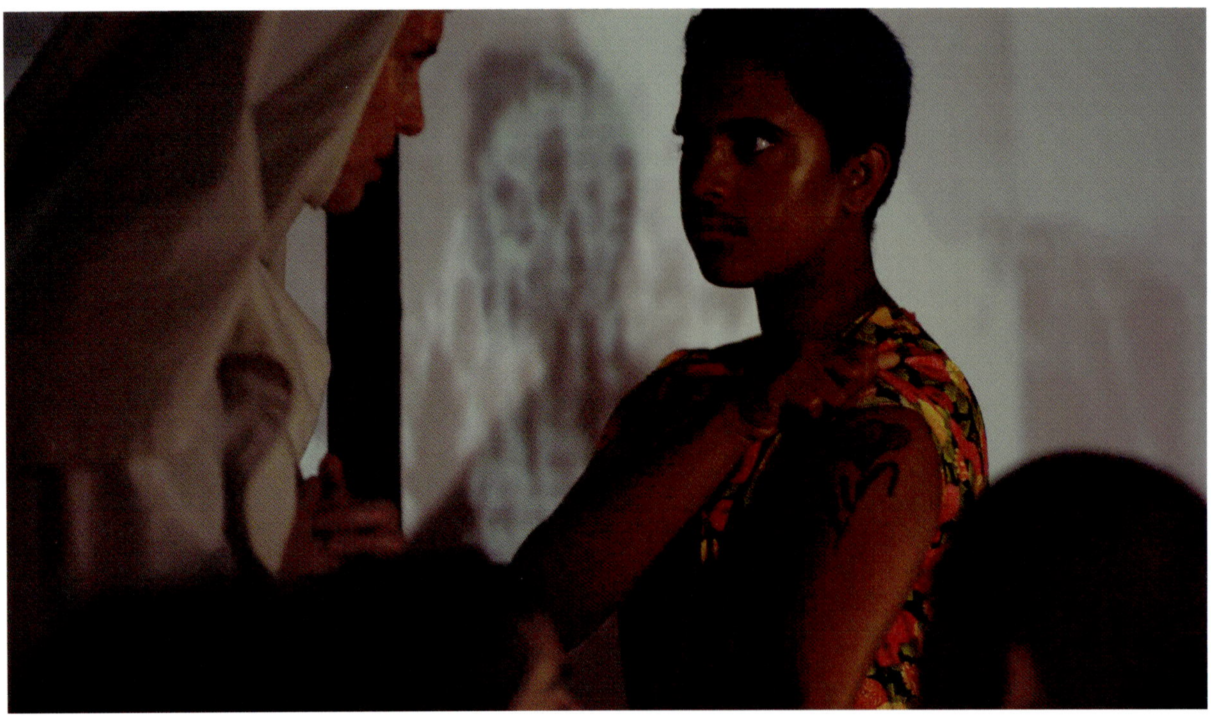

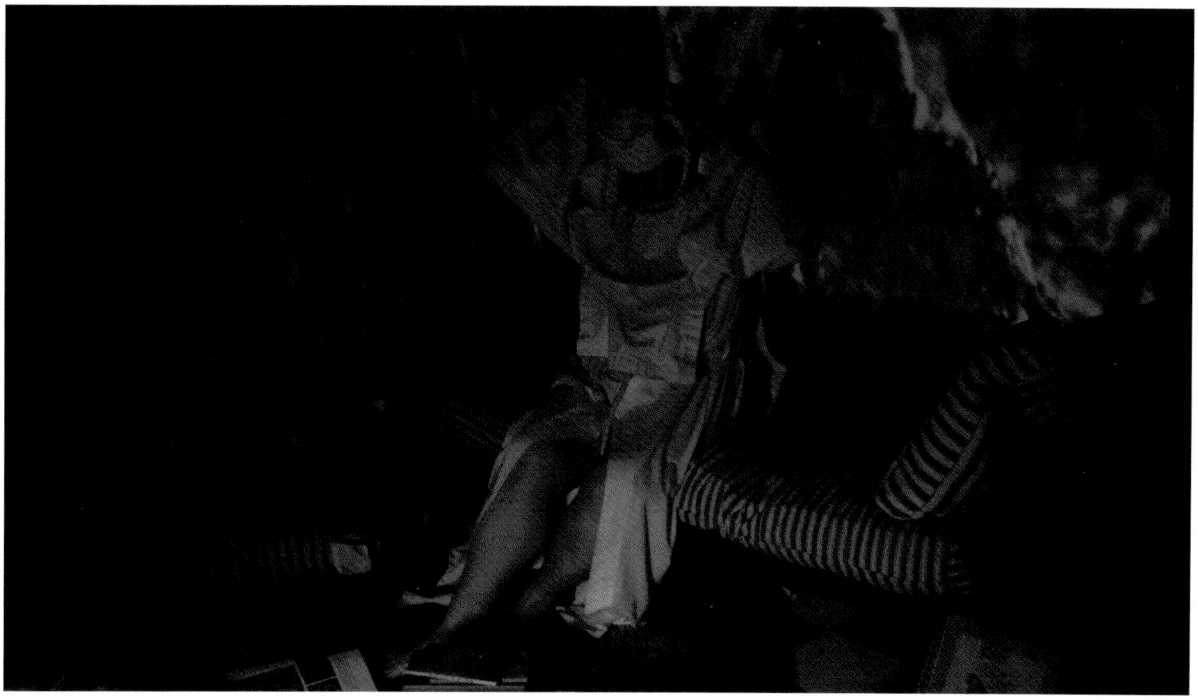

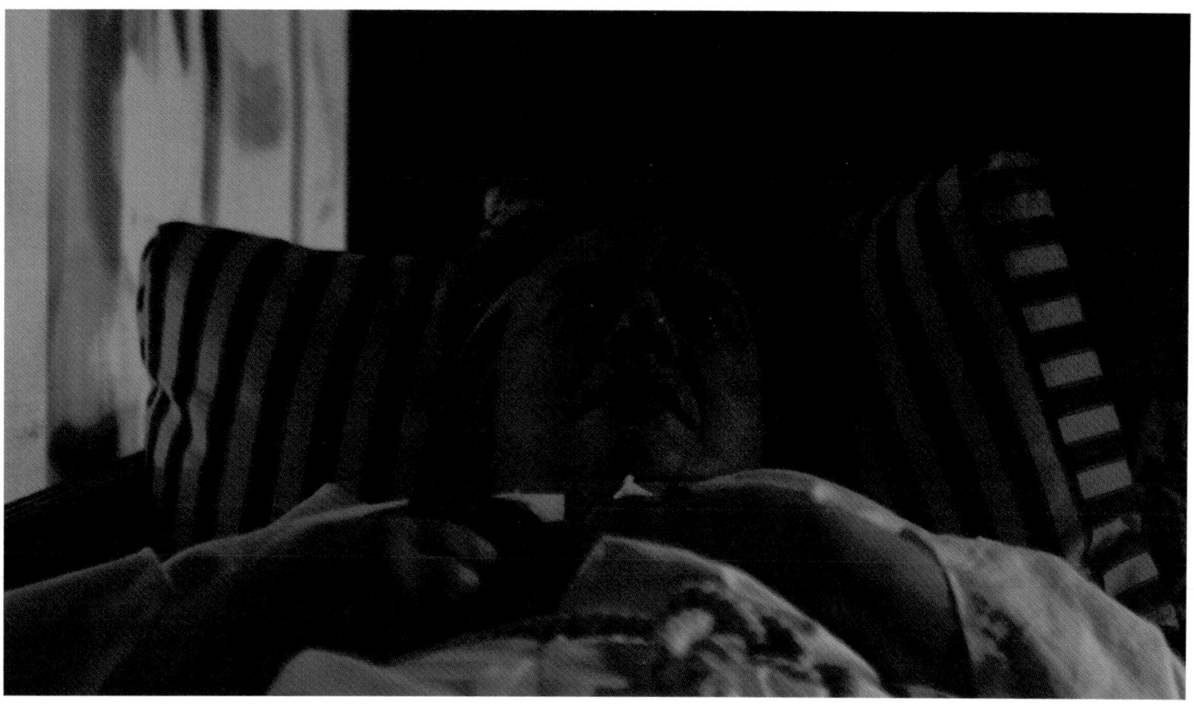

INT. STUDIO SPACE (EMPTY) - DAY 8

Sister Clodagh sits in front of a MIRROR.

She applies LIPSTICK.

She is out of her nun's habit and now in a civilian DRESS and FUR COAT.

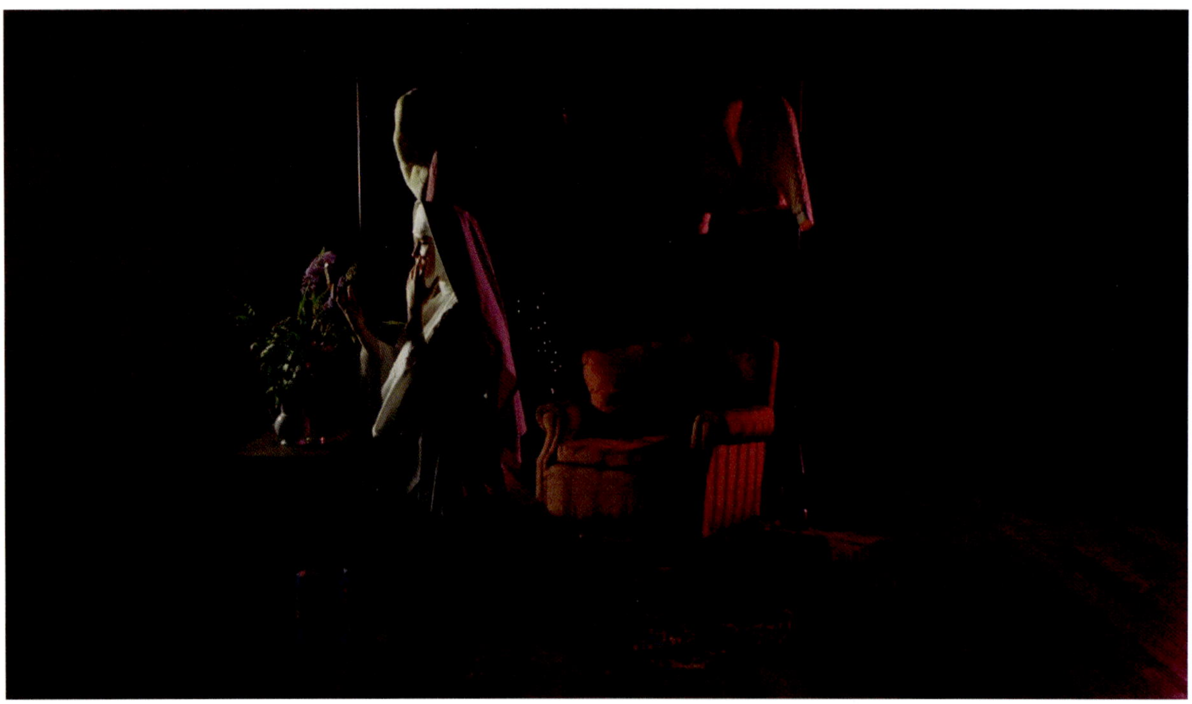

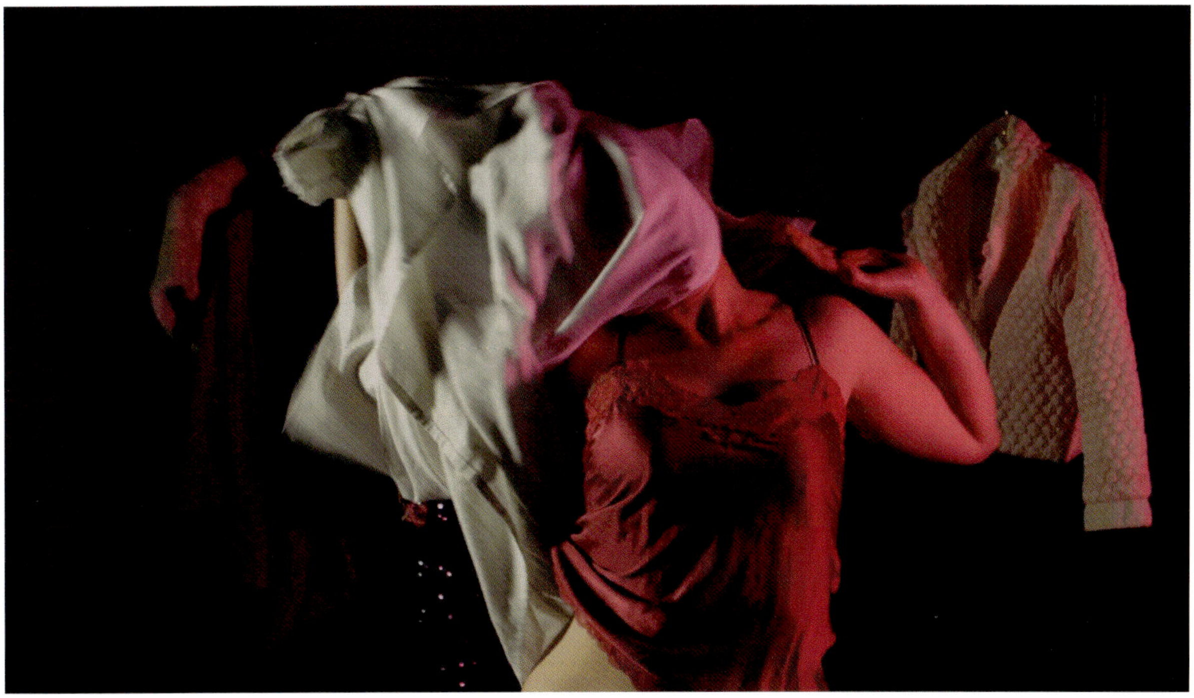

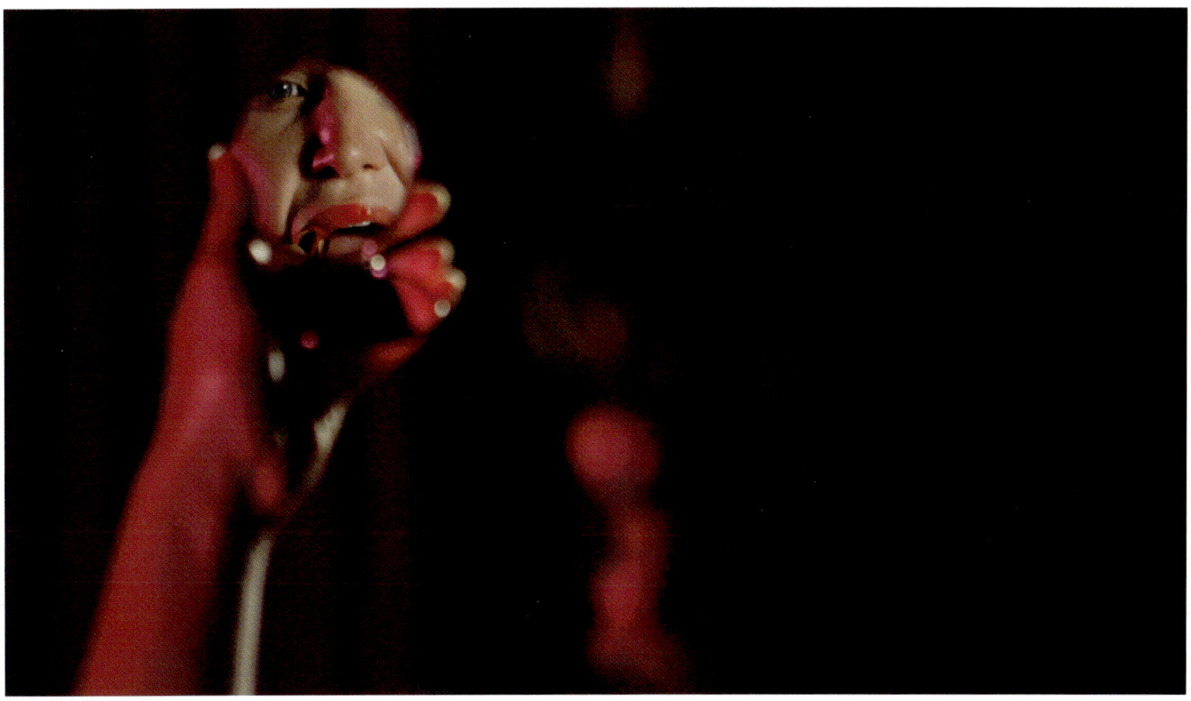

Fluid Truth

Shannon Bell

Female Ejaculation - 'shooting hot sticky liquid out of one's urethral with great velocity' (Bell, 2010, 39) - is the political female body event of the late twentieth and twenty-first centuries. That is, if politics and the political are understood the way in which Jacques Rancière understands them: as 'an intervention in the visible and the sayable' which makes 'what was unseen visible' and 'what was audible as mere noise heard as speech' (Rancière, 2010, pp. 37-8). And, if event, *a la* Alain Badiou, is taken to be an unsuspected eruption that ruptures the routine operation of power, in this case the hegemonic heterosexual male point of view and the sexuated body-politic of language and culture underpinning the knowledge of what a male and a female body can do. This essay will use key concepts formulated by French philosophers Alain Badiou and Jacques Rancière to present the truth event of female ejaculation. A not unimportant secondary objective is to show the fluid applicability of high theory to sites not imagined by the originators of the theory.

The radical feminist philosopher Catharine MacKinnon contends, 'The male perspective is systematic and hegemonic... [M]ost men adhere to it, nonconsciously and without considering it a point of view, ... because it makes sense of their experience [and] because it is in their interest. It is rational for them' (MacKinnon, 1989, p. 114). This systematic and hegemonic male perspective can be taken as equivalent to what Rancière identifies as the 'logic of *arkhê*' which 'presupposes that a determinate superiority is exercised over an equally determinate inferiority' (Rancière, 2010, p. 31). The 'logic of *arkhê*' *is* at the core of what Rancière terms 'the police', operating as the opposite of politics. He notes, 'For a political subject - and therefore for politics - to come to pass, it is necessary to break with this logic' (2010, p. 30). Politics or democracy works 'as a rupture in the logic of *arkhê*' (2010, p. 31); 'Politics', the way Rancière sees it, is:

> the activity that breaks with the order of the police by inventing new subjects ... new forms of collective enunciation ... new ways of making sense of the sensible, new configurations between the audible and the inaudible, new distributions of space and time – in short, new bodily capacities (Rancière, 2010, p. 139).

Female Ejaculator (FE) Militant Subjects

One of the political subjects that ruptures the logic of *arkhê* and the police sexual order is the ejaculating female subject, traversing the process of what Alain Badiou *a la* Jacques Lacan terms *subjectivization* - in the first instance, through a hysterical cut into, a noisy disruption, of hegemonic heterosexuality. This first cut was the body disturbances and genital mucous secretions documented by Sigmund Freud in his work with Dora and the neurasthenic female ejaculators that Richard Freiherr von Krafft-Ebing found among a female prison population and documented in *Psychopathia Sexualis*. While these subjects were not mute in terms of the noise of resistance, they were not speaking militant political subjects. Rather, they were spoken about in dominant psychoanalytic and sexological discourses. *Subjectivization*, as understood by Badiou, 'is that through which a truth is possible' (Badiou, 2005, p. 393). For Badiou there are three dimensions to a truth-process: the event, the fidelity and the truth. As Badiou states: 'For the process of truth to begin, something must happen' (Badiou, 2002, lecture). The truth process of female ejaculation began when Female Ejaculator (FE) militant subjects, such as myself and Deborah Sundahl started to and continue to speak on female ejaculation publically by teaching workshops, writing texts, producing our own films and doing documentary footage for television documentaries, such as Gilles Boyon and Segolene Hanotaux's 2011 documentary film, *G-Spotting: A Story of Pleasure and Promise.*

Female ejaculation is an *event* for feminist thought and sexuality in much the same way that 'Marx is an event for political thought because he designates, under the name "proletariat", the central void of early bourgeois societies' (Badiou, 2001, p. 69).

Bell and Sundahl, and other FE militant subjects such as Annie Sprinkle and Carol Queen, designate under the name of 'female ejaculation' the central void of female sexuality. It is this void that MacKinnon, through radical feminism, positions as the absence on which male sexuality is grounded:

> women is identified as a being who identifies and is identified as one whose sexuality exists for someone else, who is socially male. What is termed women's sexuality is the capacity to arouse desire in that someone (MacKinnon, 1989, p. 118).

MacKinnon poses the question: 'If what is sexual about a woman is what the male point of view requires for excitement, for arousal and satisfaction, have male requirements so usurped its terms to have become them?' (MacKinnon, 1989, p. 118). Consciousness-raising, the method of radical feminism, showed female sexuality under male control to be negation of self as subject: 'Man fucks woman; subject verb object' (1989, p. 124).

In 1989, the same year in which MacKinnon's *Toward a Feminist Theory of the State* was published, the ejaculating female began her collective enunciation, presenting images and texts initially inside a queer feminist discourse (See Appendix I: Female Ejaculation Event 1988-2012). This, in retrospect, became the event of female ejaculation which brought 'to pass "something other" than the situation, opinions, instituted knowledges' (Badiou, 2001, p. 67) that predominated concerning what a female body could do. The Female Ejaculation event was a 'hazardous, unpredictable supplement' (Badiou, 2001, p. 67); 'a multiple on the edge of the void' (Badiou, 2005, p. 202).

Gilles Boyon and Segolene Hanotaux's 2011 documentary film, *G-Spotting: A Story of Pleasure and Promise*, featuring footage from a workshop with me, broadcast on French and Swedish television and screened at the International Documentary Film Festival Amsterdam (IDFA) in November 2012, is one of the latest inscribing and naming of 'the situated void of that for which it is an event' (Badiou, 2001, p. 69); it is an act of fidelity. Recall that, for Badiou, the event is both situated and supplementary, never fully decidable, 'one-multiple made up of... all the multiples that belong to its site... and the event itself' (Badiou, 2005, p. 179). Fidelity 'amounts to a sustained investigation of the situation [female sexuality] under the imperative of the event [female ejaculation] itself' (Badiou, 2001, p. 67). Boyon and Hanotaux, in their promotional abstract for the IDFA screening of *G-Spotting: A Story of Pleasure and Promise*, repose their work as a fidelity to previous investigations into the G-spot and female ejaculation:

> *G-spotting* is a joyful and surprising film, with colorful characters, exploring science, sexual liberation, ideological conflicts, and of course ... pleasure. How, in 2010, can there still exist myths around female sexuality? How can the simple mention of this erogenous zone provoke such argument, doubt, and salacious laughter? How can a simple erogenous zone mysteriously denominated as the 'G-Spot' be known to all yet... no-one (or almost no-one) knows its location, its physiology or the story of its discovery? *G-spotting* is an investigation into the heart of the fascinating world of scientific sexology (IDFA, n.d.).

G-Spotting 'gathers together and produces' (Badiou, 2001, p. 68) what is now broadly accepted as the truth about female genital anatomy and the female body's capacity for female ejaculation, this time for a broader television audience. The truth of the female body's sexual capacity 'punches a "hole" in knowledges, it is heterogeneous to them, but it is also the ... source of new knowledges' (Badiou, 2001, p. 70). Badiou continues: 'We shall say that the truth *forces* knowledges' (2001, p. 70). 'Force' indicates that a new truth comes into being 'by violating established and circulating knowledges' (Badiou, 2001, p. 70). *G-Spotting* pitched by

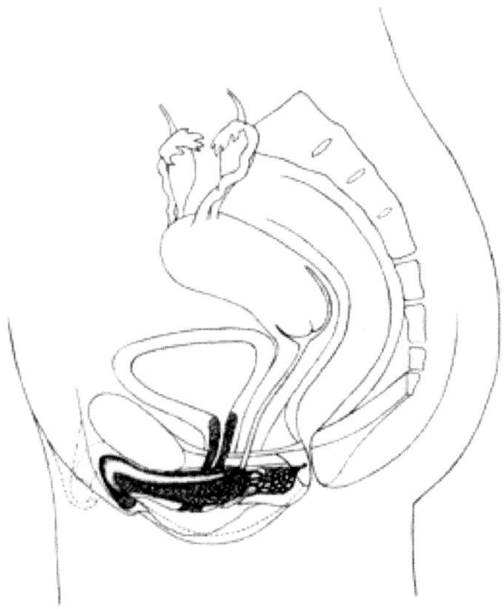

3-16 A side view of the clitoris: Compared to the penis

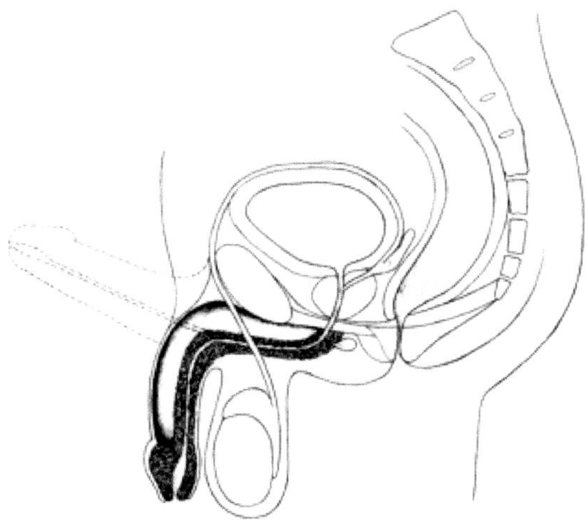

3-17 A side view of the penis. Compared to the clitoris

Boyon and Hanotaux as 'a joyful and surprising film, with colorful characters,' perhaps to sell it to television networks, is in its publicity an understated approach to 'forcing new bits of knowledge'. In the film the female body capacity for ejaculation is confirmed by Dr. Francisco Santamaria Cabello as he discusses the presence of PSA (prostate specific antigen) in female ejaculate and post-orgasm urine. Cabello's laboratory research found that all women whose pre and post-orgasm urine his team tested have PSA in urine after orgasm, even if they do not know that they ejaculate. The film transitions from Cabello's laboratory work to the FE workshops I teach, primarily at Come As Your Are (http://www.comeasyouare.com/toronto-store-information/sex-workshops/).(1) The film narrator states: 'Thanks to Cabello the field of sexology is no longer in the dark about the anatomy of squirting'. Then the narrator qualifies: 'But his discovery that all women might be capable of ejaculation is something that has been well known in some subcultures for many years'. Of course, these subcultures are queer feminist communities.

Female Ejaculation Force

I wrote the first set of instructions on how to female ejaculate in 'Q: What Shoots and Sprays, Shoots and Sprays, Shoots and Sprays? A: A Woman' published, as the feature article for the International Women's Day issue of the lesbian magazine *Rites* in 1989. The issue included black and white images of me doing two different types of female ejaculation – the spurting gush and the jet stream – and two texts, one which traced the genealogy of female ejaculation and one entitled 'The Everywoman's Guide to Ejaculation', which provided step-by-step directions on how to ejaculate:

> Step One: Find what has come to be known as your G-spot; don't call it that, it is named after Gräfenberg, a man. It is the muscle and spongy tissue around that part of your urethra that is on the top wall of your vagina. It is about half a finger (more or less) inside your vagina and about a finger across – about two inches. If the muscles that go around your vagina have not been used too much (mine weren't) they have to be built up. The muscles can be built up by doing contractions: pressing the top of your vagina against the bottom and releasing. DON'T WORRY: Strong muscles will not hold the penis in place; they will push it out when your ducts get full and you want to shoot.
>
> Step Two: Using whichever hand you usually masturbate with, take two or three fingers and rub them against the part of your urethra inside your vagina. Press hard and notice the feeling of having to pee. You don't, this is the signal that you are ready to ejaculate. Now, place the middle finger slightly below the external part of your urethra and begin to masturbate the same way you rub your clit. As you are doing this you will notice the two ducts, one at each side of your urethra, feel full and perhaps somewhat painful; you have another 30 or so ducts scattered in the urethral sponge on the top wall of your vagina. Once you get into the body feeling you may be able to locate them externally on your lower abdomen. They are located in a pyramid from your clit to just near your ovaries.
>
> Step Three: Take your other hand and press down on one or more of the ducts from the outside. Push your urethra out and push the way you do when you pee. A crucial aspect of ejaculating is that it is necessary to PUSH OUT. Liquid will come shooting out perhaps in a steady stream or jet.
>
> I can ejaculate only in positions in which I can push my entire pelvis out and up: on my knees with legs a foot and a half apart; on my back with my ass raised up, weight distributed on my feet and shoulders, and knees at least two feet apart; squatting, standing, again with feet far enough apart so I can push my urethra up and out. As a veteran ejaculator, following stimulation on my urethra and urethral sponge I can ejaculate by just pushing out.
>
> If your partner is female, you may be able to help her ejaculate. As you stimulate her anterior vaginal wall and the exterior part of her urethra, get her to push out when she is ready. You will both feel the glands and ducts around the urethra swelling and filling with liquid.

Vol. 5 #9 MARCH 89 TORONTO, CANADA • $2

RITES

FOR LESBIAN AND GAY LIBERATION

- AIDS drugs legalized at last
- Love American style: A visit to the lesbian baths of San Francisco
- AIDS education goes to school

Taking the sexual revolution one step further

Female Ejaculation

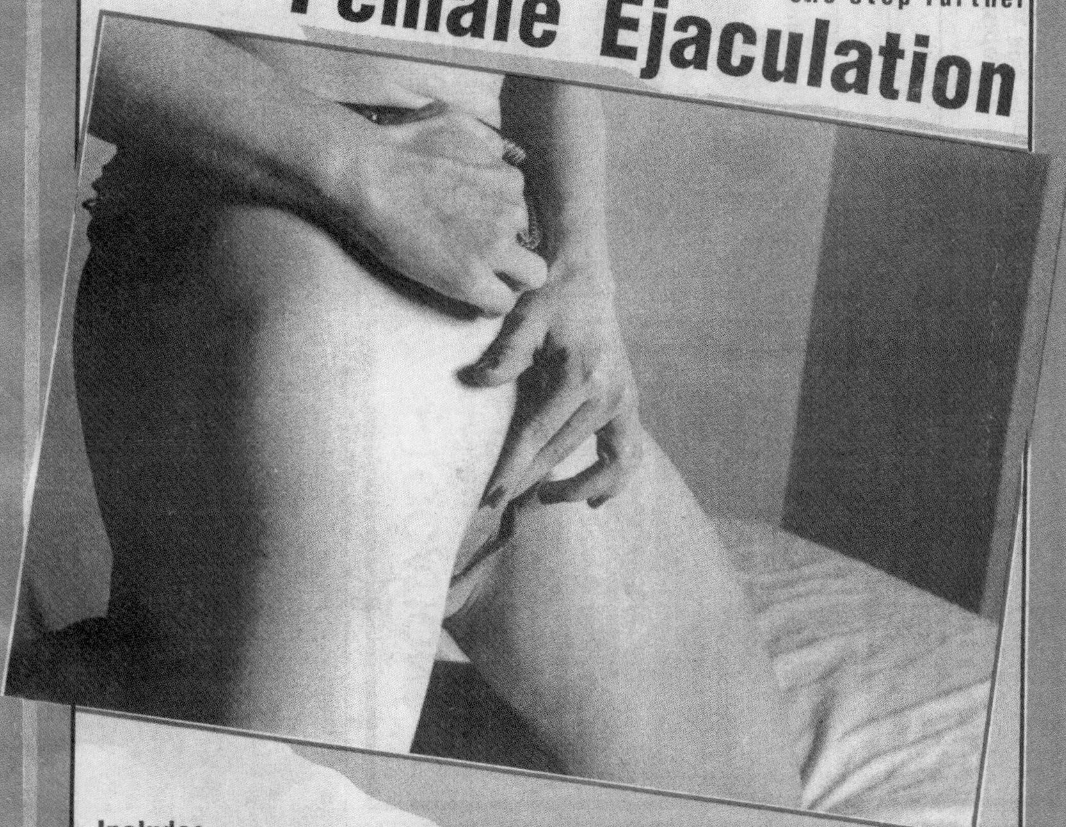

Includes step-by-step instructions!
The Everywoman's Guide to Ejaculation

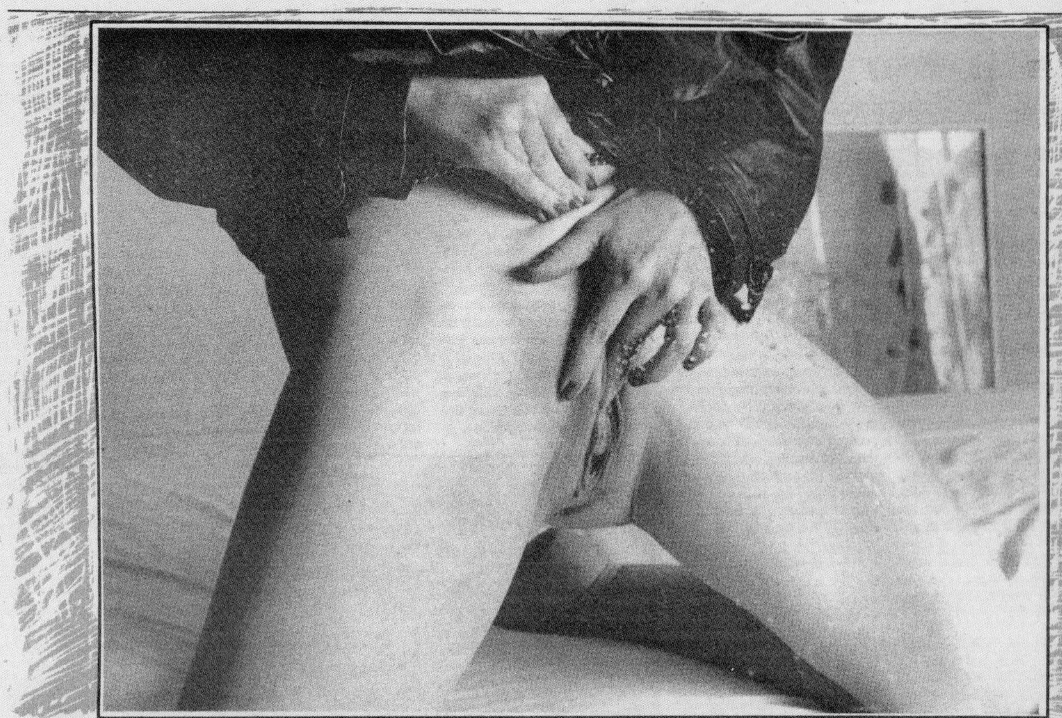

Female ejaculation, writes Shannon Bell, once thought to be a normal and pleasurable part of female sexu ity, came to be a symptom of the hysteric, the content of male phantasy and the property of the pornograp woman. *Photo by Ruthann Tucker.*

by Shannon Bell

For Gad, my partner in cum, with love.

This piece is about the ejaculating female body. How did it cum to be that male ejaculation has never been questioned, debated, analyzed; just accepted as a given feature of the male body and male sexuality? Sounds like an odd question, doesn't it? Yet it is no more odd than what has actually happened to female ejaculation throughout history.

There are two questions that have not been raised about female ejaculation from the first discussion of it by Hippocrates (460-377 B.C.) to the most recent, by Josephine Sevely, *Eve's Secrets—A New Theory of Female Sexuality* (1987). The first is: how can a woman have control over ejaculation; the second, and more recent question, is: why have feminist voices failed to speak about female ejaculation? Let me put these questions on hold while I trace some of the historical writings on the topic.

Hippocrates advocated a "two semen" theory of generation based on the belief that both male and female fluids contributed to conception. Aristotle's (384-322 B.C.) understanding of female ejaculation didn't rely on reproductive function. He located it in the realm of pleasure:

> Some think that the female contributes semen in coition because the pleasure she experiences is sometime similar to that of the male, and also is attended by a liquid discharge. But this discharge is not seminal... The amount of this discharge, when it occurs, is sometimes on a different scale from the emission of semen and far exceeds it.

Ejaculatory pleasure is recorded again by Galen, a second century Roman physician. Galen entered the controversy over whether female fluids were generative or not in support of Hippocrates. He made a distinction between female fluid which was procreative (menstrual blood) and female fluid that was pleasure-creative. The source of the latter he identified as the female prostate. DeGraaf, a 17th century Dutch anatomist, in his *New Treatise Concerning the Generative Organs of Women*, described and drew the female prostate as well as describing the female fluid.

In 1880 a physician named Skene identified two ducts inside the urethral opening which subsequently became known as the Skene glands. He was concerned with the problem of draining these glands and the ducts surrounding the female urethra when they became infected. This marks the subsequent direction of the medical profession: a concern with the Skene glands and the urethra not as sources of pleasure but as potential sites of venereal disease and infection. Evidence of female fluids became linked with disease.

Q: *What shoots and sprays, shoots and sprays, shoots and sprays?*
A: *A Woman*

Freud, following the medical convention of his time, made a connection between hysterical symptoms and the secretion of female fluids:

> The pride taken by women in the appearance of their genitals is quite a special feature of their vanity; and disorders of genitals which they think calculated to inspire feelings of repugnance or even disgust have an incredible power of humiliating them, of lowering their self-esteem, and of making them irritable, sensitive, distrustful. An abnormal secretion of the mucous membrane of the vagina is looked upon as a source of disgust.

In Victorian England, genital fluids were a source of disgust to females as well as to males. As taboo, they were relegated to the pornographic field. *The Pearl*, a two volume journal of Victorian short stories, poems, letters, and ballads, contains depictions of ejaculation. Steven Marcus, in *The Other Victorians: A Study of Sexuality and Pornography in Mid-Nineteenth Century England*, found that in pornographic writings

> there is first the ubiquitous projection of the male sexual fantasy onto the female response—the female response being imagined as identical with the male...and there is the usual accompanying fantasy that they ejaculate during orgasm.

Female ejaculation, once thought to be a normal and pleasurable part of female sexuality, came to be a symptom of the hysteric, the content of male fantasy, and the property of the pornographic woman.

The ejaculating female body, a body cheated out of its own history, is found in a love letter written in 1916 by a triply-bad bad girl, Almeda Sperry (lesbian prostitute anarchist), to a doubly-bad bad girl Emma Goldman (anarchist bisexual).

> Dearest, it is a good thing that I came away w
> At this moment I am listening to the rhythm of
> coming in your throat. I am surging along
> lifeblood, coursing in the secret places of your b
> not escape the rhythmic spurt of your love juices
> Falk, *Love, Anarchy and Emma Goldman*)

De-eroticizing Female Pleasure

Apart from a few notes by anthropologists, not
was written on female ejaculation until recent
picked it up. Kinsey mentions female ejaculati
its existence. Masters and Johnson note th
ejaculation is an erroneous but widespread con

In 1950 Grafenberg, a German obstetr
gynecologist, in an article published in *The In*
Journal of Sexology, reported his observations of
sion of female fluids from the urethra.

> An erotic zone always could be demonstra
> anterior wall of the vagina along the course of th
> Analogous to the male urethra, the female u
> seems to be surrounded by erectile tissues... In
> of sexual stimulation, the female urethra begins
> and can be felt easily. It swells out greatly at the
> gasm... Occasionally the production of fluids is.
> If there is the opportunity to observe... one can se
> quantities of a clear transparent fluid are expell
> the urethra in gushes... In the cases observed by
> was examined and it had no urinary character.

What marked subsequent writings on t
urethra, even in the late 1970s and 1980s in th
Sex Research, was not its erotic potential. A listi
of the titles if these articles should be sufficient
the de-eroticization of female ejaculatio
ejaculatory organ: "Female Ejaculation: A C
(1981); "Pelvic Muscle Strength of Female
Evidence in Support of a New Theory of Orga
"Female Ejaculation and Urinary Stress Inc
"Concentrations of Fructose in Female Ejaculate
A Comparative Biochemical Study" (1988); an
Urethral Expulsions Evoked by Local Digital S
of the G-Spot: Difference in Response Patterns."

Female ejaculation was legitimated and popu
the first time in *The G Spot and Other Recent Disco*
Female Sexuality (1982). A large portion of the
"Female Ejaculation" is composed of intervie
and case vignettes of women who ejaculate. Ma
women have been persecuted by their compani
the medical profession for "urinary incontinen

depict the act of ejaculation as an experience of pleasure and a regular part of their sexuality. The authors of the *G-Spot* suggest that because "female ejaculate can only serve one purpose: pleasure" and because women have historically been absented from the realm of pleasure, the knowledge of ejaculation has not been accepted and socially appropriated by professionals or the public.

Josephine Sevely's *Eve's Secrets—A New Theory of Female Sexuality* (1987), has provided the most comprehensive study of female ejaculation. Her theory not only sexualizes the urethra and but also emphasizes the simultaneous involvement of the clitoris, urethra, and vagina and the ways they function together as a single integrated sexual organ. She refutes the theory of male and female counterparts encoded, since Aristotle, in western philosophy and medicine, the theory that describes woman as an incomplete version of man and the female prostate and glands as vestigial male structures.

The implications of Sevely's theory are threefold: First, a woman's sexual organ ceases to be fragmented into clitoris and vagina; it is reconstructed as an integrated whole composed of clitoris, urethra, and vagina. Second, this integrated whole is "full of things," all alive with sensation. The w/hole is an active w[hole]; no more clitoral activity versus vaginal passivity. Third, it becomes clear that the anatomical difference between male and female genitals upon which phallocentric culture and society are premised is a socially constructed difference. Both male and female bodies have prostrate gland structures along the floor of the urethra and have the potential to ejaculate fluids during sexual stimulation.

The female body can ejaculate fluid from thirty-one ducts; can, with stimulation, ejaculate repeatedly; and, as well, can enjoy a plurality of genital pleasure sites: the clitoris, urethra, vagina—the vagina entrance, the roof of the vagina, the bottom of the vagina, the cervix.

When I was in New York in August 1987, Al Goldstein's (the publisher of *Screw* magazine) program on the sex channel was featuring one of New York's top porno stars. The woman was demonstrating her "squirt technique" which is featured in her films. Once again female ejaculation has emerged in the pornography industry. A male porno star went down on the woman while Al talked. When the woman was ready, the man stopped, and she masturbated herself to ejaculation/orgasm. When Goldstein interviewed the woman she said "it's psychological...I just masturbate and think real hard about squirting and when I'm ready I push out." What she failed to mention was that while she closed her eyes and was concentrating she was also pressing on her pelvis from the outside which meant she was pushing down on her urethra and vaginal roof.

Feminism and Ejaculation

The ejaculating female body has not acquired a feminist voice nor has it been part of feminist discussions, even feminist sexual discussions. What is the reason for this? It has to do with the fact that the questions posed by many feminists and the basic assumptions some feminists make about female sexuality are overwhelmingly premised on the difference between female and male bodies. The primary difference—the ability to give birth—has been emphasized as a central metaphor in feminist critiques of patriarchal texts and has been theorized into a "philosophy of birth" and an economy of reproduction. What has resulted is a definition of the female body which focuses on its reproductive capacity at the expense of its ejaculatory capacity. At the core of this silencing is a basic assumption about female sexuality. If sexuality is perceived as "one moment in the biological process of reproduction," as Mary O'Brien puts it, then the maternal female body takes precedence. If, on the other hand, reproduction is seen as one moment in the sexual process, then we give precedence to the libidinal female body. Space exists for theorizing the ejaculating female body in addition to the maternal female body and, possibly, the ejaculating maternal body. However, the power of the difference paradigm is so pervasive that even in the sex positive work of writers such as Carol Vance, Gayle Rubin, Joan Nestle and the Samois collective, female ejaculation is ignored. To accept female ejaculation one has to accept sameness and the equality of male and female bodies.

The few feminist responses to writings on female ejaculation have been tepid if not negative. The Boston Women's Health Collective, the editors of *Our Bodies, Our Selves,* caution against the G-Spot and female ejaculation being "used to reinstate so-called 'vaginal' orgasms as superior" or "becoming a new source of pressure" to perform. Barbara Ehrenreich and her co-authors, in *Remaking Love, the Feminization of Sex* misconstrue the emphasis on the urethra in *The G-Spot* as a return to Freud's primacy of the mature vaginal orgasm. They raise two criticisms. Ejaculation is something that happens if one has strong muscles. If one doesn't one must build these up by doing Kegel exercises (contraction exercises). This is construed as serving "to strengthen the muscles that hold the penis in place." Their second criticism is that "the acrobatics necessary to achieve the 'new' orgasm" privilege male-dominant sexual positions. The latter criticism is odd since Ladas and others provide case vignettes of ejaculations in many different positions: woman on top, rear entry, man on top, partner using her/his hand, and woman using her own hand. They provide case histories from lesbians and note that "preliminary reports indicate that there may be a higher incidence of female ejaculation in the lesbian population than there is among heterosexual women."

What would a body in *control* of ejaculation, a sexual body that *violates* its repression be like? To begin with one could imagine the woman ejaculating on the late night sex show to be the woman ejaculating with a sexual friend or by herself. After having her clitoris and urethra stimulated by a mouth, a hand, or a vibrator, the woman positioned on her knees with legs wide apart and pelvis tilted forward, begins to masturbate; when she feels she is ready (when her ducts feel full), she contracts her vaginal muscles and pushes her urethra out at the same time using her other hand or her friend's hand to press on her pelvis, to squeeze the liquid out of her ducts; the fluid sprays out hitting the wall (or her friend); she laughs and repeats.

Shannon Bell is a pornographic woman. Her favourite activities are ejaculating and working out. She is in the Political Science doctoral program at York University and she is working on the Prostitute Body which she likes very much—for very different reasons than het men.

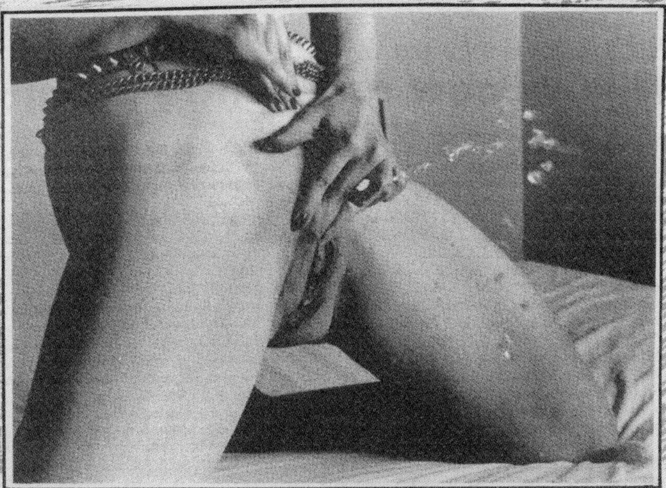

To accept female ejaculation one has to accept sameness and the equality of male and female bodies. *Photo by Ruthann Tucker.*

The Everywoman's Guide to Ejaculation

Okay, so now I know you are saying to yourself "How do I do this?" "how can I help my partner(s) do this?" "what will it do for me sexually?" "How will it empower me?" The answer to the first question, "how do I do this," is almost nowhere to be found in the sexologist literature. After attending a 1985 workshop in New York given by Alice Ladas, key author of the *G-Spot* and ejaculator, (the workshop was on the vaginal myograph and strengthening pelvic muscles), I headed for a bookstore to purchase the *G-Spot.* I read the chapter "Female Ejaculation" and I read it to Gad, then my partner and now my partner in cum. Then I started to practice. It was really difficult to figure out how to do it from the descriptions of ejaculators' experiences. For them ejaculation was something that happened not an action that they controlled. I practiced and practiced and by the time we left New York I was so sore from masturbating that I could hardly walk or pee. This was not the thrill I had expected. So I sat down again with these women's experiences and took notes. And I realized that they had not emphasized the crucial aspects about ejaculating: it is necessary to *PUSH OUT.*

Step One: Find what has come to be known as your "G-Spot"; don't call it that, it is named after Grafenberg, a man. What it is is the muscle and spongy tissue around that part of your urethra that is inside your vagina. It is about half a finger (more or less) inside your vagina and about a finger long across—about two inches. If the muscles that go around your vagina have not been used too much (mine weren't) they have to be built up. The muscles can be built up by doing contractions: pressing the top of your vagina against the bottom and releasing. This is fun and you could have an orgasm or two. You could start by doing 25 contractions three times a day for one week; then 50 three times a day, then 100. For any of you who have dildoes or penises in your vagina, don't worry: strong muscles will not hold the penis in place; they will push it out when your ducts get full and you want to shoot.

Step Two: Using whichever hand you usually masturbate with, take two or three fingers and rub them against the part of your urethra *inside* your vagina. Press hard and notice the feeling of having to pee. You don't, this is the signal that you are ready to ejaculate. Now, place the middle finger slightly below the *external* part of your urethra and begin to masturbate the same way you rub your clit. As you are doing this you will notice that the two ducts, one at each side of your urethra, feel full and perhaps somewhat painful; you have another 29 ducts scattered over the top of your vagina. Once you get into the body feeling you will be able to locate them on your lower abdomen. They are located in a pyramid from your clit to just above your ovaries.

Step Three: Take your other hand and press down on one or more of the ducts from the *outside.* Push your urethra out and push the way you do when you pee. Liquid will come shooting out perhaps in a steady stream or jet.

I can ejaculate only in positions in which I can push my entire pelvis out and up: on my knees with legs a foot and a half apart; on my back with my ass raised up, weight distributed on my feet and shoulders, and knees at least two feet apart; squatting; standing, again with feet far enough apart so I can push my urethra up and out. As a veteran ejaculator, following stimulation on my urethra I can ejaculate by just pushing out.

In response to "how can I help my partner to do this": get her to push out as you stimulate her interior and exterior urethra.

What it will do for you sexually is to give you a powerful kinesthetic, visual, and auditory experience—a total body experience. You can repeat it almost indefinitely once your body awakens to it. Seeing and hearing your body fluid put out fire gives one a whole new relation to the environment. As the fluid sprays out of your body you will feel a complete sexual release.

The ejaculate changes in amount, colour, odour, and taste during your menstrual cycle. At ovulation the fluid is very hot (it corresponds to your vaginal temperature), thick, yellowish, and pungent. Following ovulation the fluid is thinner, there is more of it, it is clear, and pleasantly salty. It remains this way until bleeding starts at which point it is again thick for the first day or so. It then returns to being clear and copious. I have also found that ejaculating during ovulation—because it reduces vaginal temperature—reduces yeast infections that result from the increase in vaginal temperature at ovulation.

> What ejaculation will do for you sexually is to give you a powerful kinesthetic, visual, and auditory experience – a total body experience. You can repeat it almost indefinitely once your body awakens to it. Seeing and hearing your body fluid put out fire gives one a whole new relation to the environment.
>
> The ejaculate changes in amount, color, odor and taste during your menstrual cycle. At ovulation the fluid is very hot (it corresponds to your vaginal temperature), thick, yellowish and pungent. Following ovulation the fluid is thinner, there is more of it, it is clear and pleasantly salty. It remains this way until bleeding starts at which point it is again thick for the first day or so. It then returns to being clear and copious. I have found that ejaculation during ovulation – because it reduces vaginal temperature – reduces yeast infections that result from the increase in vaginal temperature at ovulation.(2)

Later in 1989, filmmaker Kath Daymond and I did *Nice Girls Don't Do It*, the first film specifically on female ejaculation.(3) It was a 13-minute truth pastiche of knowledge, porn and technical instruction.

This is not to say that female ejaculation did not exist before the end of the 1980s. On the contrary, female ejaculation has a long history. Following the 1980s queer feminist female ejaculation event this history has been retrospectively reformulated as the popular culture genealogical fidelity of female ejaculation. Make no mistake, if queer feminist political militants had not ruptured the old order of female sexuality with new knowledge and practices, female ejaculation would not be an event. Rather, female ejaculation would have continued to suffer the fate of what Michel Foucault termed 'subjugated knowledge': it would appear for a moment now and then in a specific discourse (philosophy, medicine, pornography, sexology) only to be submerged out of view for extended periods of time throughout history.

Postevental Genealogical Fidelity of Female Ejaculation.(4)

Female ejaculation has been the object of medical and philosophical discourses since the early Greeks, with the meanings ascribed to it varying considerably over the course of Western history. Female ejaculation has typically been framed in five ways: as fecundity; sexual pleasure; social deviance; medical pathology; and as a scientific problem. Aristotle, in the *Generation of Animals*, connected female fluid with pleasure:

> Some think that the female contributes semen in coition because the pleasure she experiences is sometimes similar to that of the male, and also is attended by a liquid

discharge. But this discharge is not seminal... The amount of this discharge when it occurs is sometimes on a different scale from the emission of semen and far exceeds it (1912, II, 28a).

The expulsion of female fluids during sexual excitement was taken by many pre-Enlightenment thinkers to be a normal and pleasurable part of female sexuality. Well into the eighteenth century, what cultural historian Thomas Laqueur terms the 'one-sex model' predominated. In this model, male and female are seen as versions of one another, both in the anatomical sense that the vagina is an internal penis, and in the physiological sense that the fluids in men and women are interchangeable.(5) Perhaps the greatest controversy within the one-sex model was between one-seed and two-seed theories of generation, which revolved around whether female fluids were progenitive. Hippocrates and Galen argued for the existence of the female seed, Aristotle that the fluid was pleasurable but not progenitive (Laqueur, 1990, pp. 40-2).

Throughout the Middle Ages, Western scholars remained faithful to Hippocrates and Galen's notion of female sperm, which came to them through Arabic medicine. In the sixteenth century, Italian anatomist Renaldus Columbus linked the clitoris with semen, ejaculation and pleasure: 'If you rub it vigorously with a penis, or touch it even with a little finger, semen swifter than air flies this way and that on account of the pleasure' (cited in Laqueur, 1990, p. 66). Female-to-female instruction is present in seventeenth-century whore dialogue, an early genre of erotic writing that combines pornographic tales with educational instruction in which an older woman teaches a young virgin about the female sex organ. In a dialogue between Tullia and her younger cousin Octavia, they discuss female ejaculation:

Tullia: Towards the upper Part of the C_t, is a thing they call Clitoris; which is a little like a Man's P___k, for it will send forth a Liquor, which when it comes away, leaves us in a Trance, as if we were dying, all our Senses being lost, and our Eyes shut[.]

Octavia: You describe Things so exactly, that me thinks I see all that is within me (Chorier, [1660.], p. 11–12).

The seventeenth-century Dutch anatomist Regnier de Graaf, in his *New Treatise Concerning the Generative Organs of Women*, outlined the Hippocratic and Aristotelian controversy over female semen, in which he sided with the Aristotelians and denied the existence of female semen. In describing the ejection of female fluid, de Graaf wrote: 'it should be noted that the discharge from the female prostatae causes as much pleasure as does that from the male prostatae' ([1672], p. 107). He identified the source of the fluid as the 'ducts and lacunae...

around the orifice of the neck of the vagina and the outlet of the urinary passage [which] receive their fluid from the female prostatae, or rather the thick membranous body around the urinary passage' ([1672], p. 107). De Graaf was the first person to name and describe the female prostate (Zaviacic, 1999, p. 17).

As the similarities between male and female bodies gave way to their differences, and semen became the sole property of the male body, the capacity of the female body to ejaculate - although still present and documented in medical writings and literature - was predominantly described as a less-than-normal occurrence.

By the nineteenth century, female fluids were linked with disease. Alexander Skene, who in 1880 identified the two ducts on each side of the urethral opening, was concerned with the problem of draining the glands and the ducts surrounding the female urethra when they became infected. The Skene glands and the urethra hence became important to the medical profession as potential sites of venereal disease and infection, and not as loci of pleasure.

The ejaculation of female fluids also came to be associated with a deviant sexual population and practice. In Richard Freiherr von Krafft-Ebing's well-known study of sexual perversion, *Psychopathia Sexualis*, he identifies female ejaculation as the pathology of a lesbian subgroup within a deviant group - the female prison population. Under the heading of 'Congenital Sexual Inversion in Women', Krafft-Ebing discusses sexual contact among women. He writes: 'The intersexual gratification among ... women seems to be reduced to kissing and embraces, which seems to satisfy those of weak sexual instinct, but produces in sexually neurasthenic females ejaculation' ([1886] 1965, p. 265).

According to Krafft-Ebing, ejaculation only occurs among women who suffer neurasthenia – body disturbances (or orgasms) - caused by weakness of the nervous system. Krafft-Ebing relates female ejaculation to a nervous disability, a feature corroborated by Freud in his analysis of Dora. Freud makes a connection between Dora's hysterical symptoms and the secretion of female fluids, and links 'abnormal secretions' with hysteria.

> The pride taken by some women in the appearance of their genitals is quite a special feature of their vanity; and disorders of genitals which they think calculated to inspire feelings of repugnance or even disgust have an incredible power of humiliating them, of lowering their self-esteem... An abnormal secretion of the mucous membrane of the vagina is looked upon as a source of disgust (Freud, [1905], p. 121).

As female ejaculation was being pathologised by the medical profession, psychoanalysis and the burgeoning sexology industry, female ejaculation surfaced in Victorian male pornographic discourse. *The Pearl*, a two-volume journal of Victorian short stories, poems, letters and ballads, contains depictions of female ejaculation misinterpreted by Steven Marcus in *The Other Victorians* as 'the ubiquitous projection of the male sexual fantasy onto the female response - the female response being imagined as identical with the male... and there is the usual accompanying fantasy that they ejaculate during orgasm' (1966, p. 194).

The clearest and most complete description of the physiological process and anatomical structure of female ejaculation was published in the *International Journal of Sexology* (1950) by Ernst Gräfenberg, a German obstetrician and gynecologist. Gräfenberg observed that:

> An erotic zone always could be demonstrated on the anterior wall of the vagina along the course of the urethra... Analogous to the male urethra, the female urethra also seems to be surrounded by erectile tissues... In the course of sexual stimulation, the female urethra begins to enlarge and can be felt easily. It swells out greatly at the end of orgasm... Occasionally the production of fluids... [is] profuse... If there is the opportunity to observe... one can see that large quantities of a clear transparent fluid are expelled... out of the urethra in gushes (1950, p. 148).

Despite the descriptions of it in medical, philosophical and pornographic literature throughout Western history, and in spite of Gräfenberg's work, female ejaculation was ignored or denied by the dominant discourses - in Rancière's terms, the discourses of the police order - defining female sexuality until the 1980s. This preevental genealogy of female ejaculation had been one of discovery, disappearance and rediscovery reclaimed and popularised after the event.

Female Ejaculation: The Event(6)

What happened in the 1980s was the feminist sexual equivalent of the Apostle Paul's conversion on the road to Damascus. The hysterics of Dora *et al.* converts into the politics of Bell *et al.*; the hysterical subject converts into the militant subject. While female bodies have ejaculated throughout history, Female Ejaculation was not a truth-event until it was enunciated in multiple sites of queer feminist discourse that collectively and retrospectively rendered obsolete the hegemonic markings of the female body as submissive to the pleasures and desires of the male body. As Badiou notes, 'the event renders prior markings obsolete' (2003, p. 23).

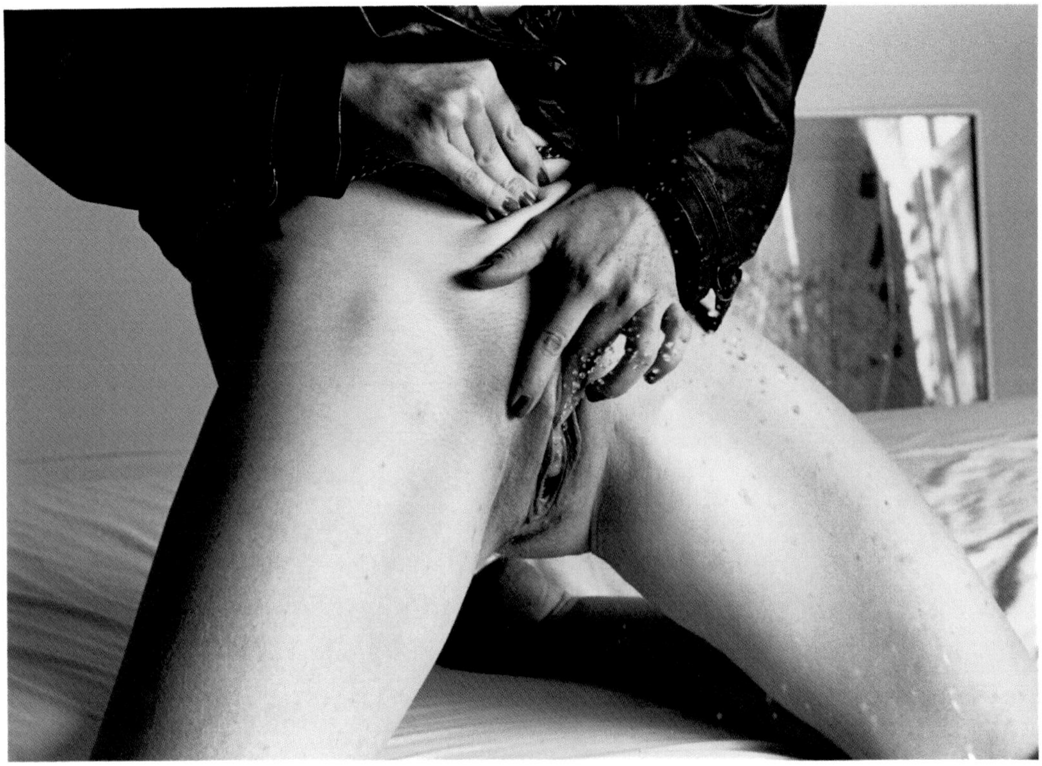

Female ejaculation is an incredibly powerful experience and image of the sexual female body. To see fluid shooting with velocity and force out of the glands and ducts that surround the urethra - what is called the 'urethral sponge' of the clitoris, now officially the 'female prostate' - through the vaginal opening, provides a new script for female sexuality and repositions the female body as powerful, active and autonomous. Female ejaculation educator Deborah Sundahl suggests, '[t]his is connectable to a broadening of women's social and sexual roles' (Bell, 1995, p. 273). I say, '[t]he visual image of female ejaculation relieves the phallus of its patriarchal burden' (1995, pp. 273-4).

A New Female Body

The paradigm shift in knowledge about and representations of female sexuality began with *A New View of a Woman's Body* (1981), compiled by the Federation of Feminist Women's Health Centers (FWHC), which in a brilliant political move redefined the clitoris, extending its visible external structure, the glans of the clitoris, to incorporate the internal spongy erectile tissue on the top and bottom vaginal walls. The FWHC named the tissue on the top wall of the vagina the 'urethral sponge' and the spongy tissue on the bottom wall, the 'perineal sponge' (1991, pp. 43–5). During sexual excitement, the urethral and perineal sponges become engorged and erect; the paraurethral glands and ducts in the urethral sponge fill with prostatic and other fluid which can be ejaculated through the urethra. From Badiou's point of view this shift would not constitute simply a new view of a pre-existing body; rather, it would constitute a new body, something like the manner in which the church is the newly reconstituted body of Christ for Paul the Apostle.

The FWHC's *A New View of a Woman's Body* provided drawings of the clitoral structure in flaccid and erect states. These drawings make apparent the similarity in size and structure of the male and female sex organs. Directed by Mary Jane Sherfey's 1972 point-by-point comparison of clitoral and penile anatomy, the FWHC rediscovered and defined the female clitoris pragmatically through consciousness-raising sessions and shared intimate experiences which included participants taking off their clothes to compare genital anatomy and documenting each other masturbating. By doing so they acquired the practical knowledge presented in Suzann Gage's now-famous anatomical illustrations of the urethral sponge of the clitoris, complete with erectile tissue and paraurethral glands and ducts (Chalker, 2000, pp. 33–4).

In *The G-Spot* (1981), Alice Ladas, Beverly Whipple and John Perry extended the paradigm shift of the new view of the female body into the realm of heterosexual popular culture, coining the term 'G-spot' after Gräfenberg to refer to the urethral sponge. The G-spot had wider currency than the urethral sponge as it implies a secret spot that, once located, will unleash the female body's possibilities for pleasure.

The authors describe the G-spot as 'a spot inside the vagina that is extremely sensitive to deep pressure. It lies on the anterior wall of the vagina... when properly stimulated, the Gräfenberg spot swells and leads to orgasm in many women' (1981, pp. 21–2). *The G-Spot* makes two significant contributions to contemporary studies on female ejaculation: 1) it presents the female sexual organ as a unified organ, leaving behind the artificial division of the female genitals into clitoris and vagina which was so popular with Freud, Kinsey and Masters and Johnson, in which either vaginal or clitoral orgasms were privileged; and 2) it popularises female ejaculation, although it doesn't disclose how to do it.

The third key contribution - though first chronologically - to the paradigm shift in understanding and representing the female sex organ was by Josephine Sevely, who in 1978 coauthored with J. W. Bennett the first article on female ejaculation and the female prostate, 'Concerning Female Ejaculation and the Female Prostate', in the *Journal of Sex Research*. Sevely and Bennett claimed that the tissue surrounding the female urethra was the same as that surrounding the male urethra and contained thirty or more prostatic glands. They also provided the lost genealogy of female ejaculation, from ancient philosophy and medicine until 1950s sexology.

Sevely extended her theories about female sexuality into *Eve's Secrets* (1987), but it never achieved the popularity of *The G-Spot*. *Eve's Secrets* emphasizes the simultaneous involvement of the clitoris, urethra and vagina (the CUV) as a single integrated sex organ. The implications of this theory are twofold: first, a woman's sexual organ is viewed as an integrated whole, not split between clitoral activity and vaginal passivity; second, the 'anatomical alternative' between male and female genitals is challenged by a 'new' construction of anatomical symmetry. Both female and male bodies have prostate gland structures and both have the potential to ejaculate fluids during sexual stimulation. The female body can ejaculate fluid from thirty or more ducts and with stimulation it can ejaculate repeatedly. It can ejaculate more fluid than the male body and enjoy a plurality of genital pleasure sites: the clitoris, urethra, vagina, the vaginal entrance, the top and bottom walls of the vagina and the cervix.

We now know that the female sex organ is identical to the male's in structure and function – that is, the urethral sponge is capable of anywhere from a three to eight inch erection, measures a handful in circumference, and that prostatic and other bodily fluids are ejaculated from the paraurethral glands and ducts through the urethra. What then is it that prevents recognition of body symmetry and body equality? Quite likely a large part of this lack of recognition is due to the historical invisibility of the female sex organ as an integrated unit and the subsequent lack of symmetry in our male-dominated cultures of naming, or the symbolic encoding of the female and male sex organs.

Terminology is important. Milan Zaviacic, professor of Pathology and Forensic Medicine at the Comenius University of Bratislava in Slovakia, fought for twenty years to get the International Committee on Anatomical Terminology to recognise the female prostate as a functioning anatomical structure:

> It appears to be illogical to use the term prostate for the tissue in the male and a different term (Skene's glands and ducts of paraurethral glands and ducts) for the same tissue in the female. The use of the term Skene's paraurethral glands and ducts wrongly implies that

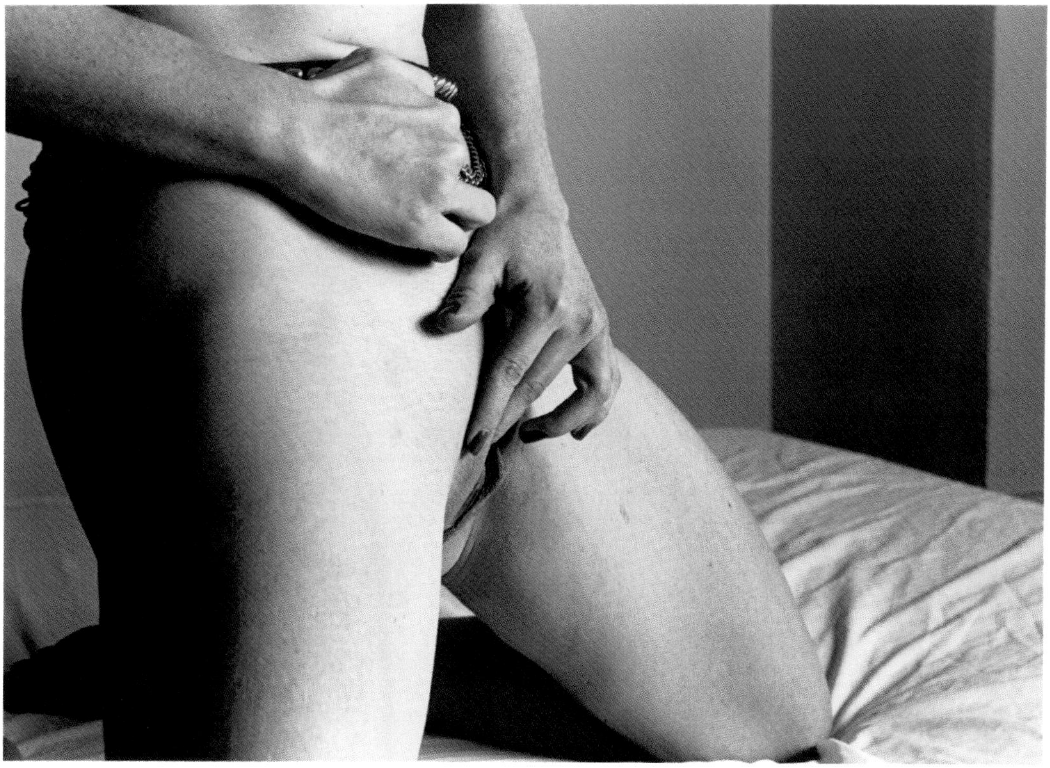

some other structure rather than the prostate is involved (Zaviacic, 1999, p. 120).

Naming is important. There are significant power differentials inherent in the naming of the female sex organ: alternately the urethral sponge, G-spot, female prostate and what I choose to name it - the female phallus.(7)

In the video *How to Female Ejaculate* (1992), Sundahl conducts a cervical self-examination. She shows the internal erection by turning the speculum sideways and inserting it inside the vagina. It is only with the turning of the speculum that the full internal and external clitoris becomes fully visible, thus also turning the female sex from the absence of 'nothing to see' into the presence of 'something to see'. The speculum, a technology developed by gynecologists to facilitate viewing of the cervix, simultaneously exposes the neck of the womb and obscures the female phallus. That is, until it is turned. The feminist turn of the technology for viewing a woman's sex generates a whole new truth of the female body, a whole new female body.

Something to See: Making the Unseen Visible

Lying down on the floor, my cunt elevated on a plush red pillow, I turned the speculum sideways and slipped it inside. Tejal, the stunningly handsome boy/girl host, illuminated my erection with a flashlight as the twenty or so Mumbai dykes, femmes and transmen looked at what was once 'nothing to see'. Some slipped on a surgical glove and slid a couple of fingers inside to stimulate my swelling hardness. The consensus was that although everyone had previously felt the female phallus in full and partial fisting activities, its visual magnitude had previously remained invisible.

The visibility of the internal erection repositions the top wall of the vagina, specifically the spongy erectile tissue and the glands and ducts surrounding the urethra, as a female phallus. It turns out that the phantom female cock haunting psychoanalysis is an actual cock; Freud's little girls' so-called hallucinations were actually body-knowledge of the presence of a real penis, always already there, awaiting the appropriate technology and action - a turned speculum - to come into view.

Female Ejaculation Dissensus in Consensus

If you Google female ejaculation, as I just did on 1 March 2014, approximately 7,350,000 results come up; on 1 March 2018, approximately 7,540,000 results come up. I always argued that once female ejaculation entered queer feminist discourse, its knowledge would never be lost again and indeed it hasn't been. What I did not foresee was the appropriation of female ejaculation into dominant heterophallic discourses reinforcing a 'male-centered, heteronormative model of human sexuality' (Chalker, 2000, p. 14).

On the one hand, there is something magnificent and fantastic about the virtual explosion of ejaculation knowledge; however, perhaps in much of this knowledge, fidelity to the pure power of female ejaculation is missing, especially if female ejaculation is presented as something one can make woman do and/or a sexual act that enhances the desire of the other. MacKinnon contends: 'Anything women have claimed as their own – motherhood, athletics, traditional men's jobs, lesbianism, feminism – is made specifically sexy, dangerous, provocative, punished, made men's in pornography' (1989, pp. 138–9), and I would add, in sexology. At one end of this male-stream continuum are males who demand ejaculation in their face as evidence of a hot sexual encounter. At the other extreme are those who have 'emotional issues' with ejaculation – they can't stand the mess, odor or power. Male sexologists busy themselves with analysing the fluid, inventing gadgets for sighting the erect urethral sponge, producing cross-sections of the urethral glands and its ducts and rediscovering the female prostate.

Pornography and sexology sites of knowledge tend to be heterophallic, diminishing female ejaculation by portraying it as yet another activity that the female body can engage in for the exotic spectacle and pleasure of her real or cyber male partners, and, moreover, as something that the in-the-know man should be able to 'facilitate' in his partner. As sociologist Ken Plummer points out, '[m]ost stories that "take off" in a culture do so because they slot easily into the most accepted narratives of that society: the dominant ideological code' (1995, p. 115).

In Rancière's terms, the 'logic of arkhê' re-solidifies; politics is reduced to consensus when female ejaculation is encoded inside old representative regimes. Yet the fluid beauty and power of female ejaculation ruptures the representative regime in which it has been positioned. In any porn or sexology site there is a *dissensus*, a conflict between the sensory ejaculating female body and that particular regime's way of making sense of it; 'a conflict between *sense* and *sense*' (Rancière, 2010, p. 139, original emphasis). Extreme sex site FuckingMachines.com, for example, makes this blatantly obvious. On the one hand, you have the opening blurb:

> Fucking Machines is machines fucking squirting pussies with extreme insertions.
>
> FuckingMachines.com is where you'll find women fucked by huge dildos strapped to sex machines that fuck hard, featuring real female orgasms and girls squirting cum. Hardcore machine fucking guarantees that hot girls get off, with custom built sex machines designed for one purpose: to make women cum hard. Experienced porn star sluts and first time girls get fucked by robotic sex machines and hard cock on camera in high definition with downloads or streaming video at speeds up to 350 RPM (Kink.com, 2013).

On the other hand, the site exposes the campiness of hegemonic porn discourse by stating that it is 'the machines [that] fuck the squirt right out of the girls pussies'. Squirt Olympics star Sindee Jennings 'cums a rocket streams of squirt and over 10-feet shot' and every machine is 'at full speed' (Kink.com, 2009). There is not a little hot irony in women talking dirty to steel: 'Fuck, fuck, bastard, shit, fuck me'. Oddly, the absence of the carbon-based, prone-to-malfunction male porn prop goes practically unnoticed. The women's performance, however, is record setting: the top squirt distance is 16 feet, speed is determined by how long the contestant can keep the hyper-metal machine stars going at full throttle, 350 RPM, before expulsion, and at the ejaculate filling-station women have one minute to fill a pint (Kink.com, 2009).

The action-image of female ejaculation is a spectacular rupturing of almost any hegemonic porn discourse in which it is located, producing a conflict between sensory regimes - that is, between representation grounded in the hegemonic 'logic of arkhê' and the aesthetic regime of politics that makes visible a new truth, in this case, a new truth about what a female body can do. This 'rupture in the relationship between *sense* and *sense*' – between what is enacted and what is seen, 'between what is seen and what is thought, and between what is thought and what is felt' (Rancière, 2010, p. 143) (porn viewer thought: she is doing it for me) - is so pronounced that, I would argue, female ejaculation - shooting hot sticky liquid out of the glands and ducts that surround one's urethra, through the urethra, with great velocity, again and again and again, trumping the male body again and again, hyperdeflating the prized male money shot in porn, flooding the image market with female fluid - breaks any 'regime of meaning' (Rancière, 2010, p. 144) in which it finds itself. The very sight of female ejaculation puts sexuated male and female bodies at risk: corporeal bodies of multiple genders have the same erectile and ejaculatory capacities.

Acknowledgements

Fluid Truth was originally published in *InterAlia. A Journal of Queer Studies* special issue *Bodily Fluids*, edited by Kamillea Aghtan, Michael O'Rourke and Karin Sellberg, #9 (2014), 49-71.
http://interalia.org.pl/en/artykuly/2014_9.htm

Thank-you to Gad Horowitz for his expert editing skills and turns of theoretical phrase, and to Raan Matalon for assisting in theorising aspects of Badiou and Rancière's work.

Endnotes

1. Female Ejaculation and The G-Spot Workshop With Shannon Bell.
Shannon Bell is one of the first producers and image creators of Female Ejaculation. Unique among female ejaculation pioneers is Shannon Bell's focus on demonstrating the extreme power and technique of female ejaculation in a safe and fun atmosphere. This popular workshop begins with a live demonstration followed by a fast female ejaculation genealogy. Bell will conclude with anatomy, step-by-step instructions, positions, toys, communication between partners as well as answer any participant's questions. Join us for an enlightening and inspiring tour that finally contextualizes both personal and historical g-spot (female phallus) knowledge. People of all genders and orientations welcome.
Wednesday, April 30, 2014. 7:30-9:30PM
Where: Come As You Are
Cost:$30/person (Sliding Scale Available)
Learn more about Female Ejaculation and The G-Spot Workshop.
$30.00
2. This originally appeared as a monologue in the video *Nice Girls Don't Do It* and was first published as 'The Everywoman's Guide to Ejaculation' in *Rites* 5(9) for 19 March 1989.

3. The earliest feminist representation of female ejaculation was part of a larger lesbian erotic film, *Clips*, produced by Blush Entertainment Group (1988).
4. This section is developed from Chapter 2, 'The Female Phallus: Something to See', of my book *Fast Feminism* (New York: Autonomedia, 2010, pp. 48-53)
5. Thomas Laqueur, featured in *Ideas* (1995). Laqueur (1990) is the author *of Making Sex: Body and Gender From The Greeks to Freud* (Cambridge and London: Harvard University Press).
6. This section is developed from 'The Female Phallus: Something to See', Chapter Two of my book *Fast Feminism* (2010), 53–6.
7. The female phallus is a different story. See Chapter 2 of my book *Fast Feminism*, 'The Female Phallus: Something to See' (2010, pp. 53–6)

Appendix I: Female Ejaculation Event 1988-2012

Film: Fatale Video, *Clips* (1988); Kath Daymond, *Nice Girls Don't Do It* (1989/90); Fatale Video, *How to Female Ejaculate* (1992); Annie Sprinkle, *Sluts and Goddesses Video Workshop* (1992); House of Chicks (Dorrie Lane), *The Magic of Female Ejaculation* (1992); Deborah Sundahl, *Tantric Journey to Female Ejaculation: Unveiling the G-Spot and Female Ejaculation* (1998); Deborah Sundahl, *Female Ejaculation for Couples* (2004); Deborah Sundahl, *Female Ejaculation: The Workshop* (2009); Deborah Sundahl, *Female Ejaculation: The Lecture* (2012); and Gilles Boyon and Segolene Hanotaux, *G Spotting: A Story of Pleasure and Promise* [documentary featuring workshop with Shannon Bell] (2011), screened at the International Documentary Film Festival, November 2012. Audio: CBC radio, *Ideas,* "One Sex or Two?" (1995). Print: I have published articles and pictures in a number of porn magazines: *Rites* (1989); *Bad Attitudes* (1992); *Lickerish* (1993); *Cupido* (1990); *Spectator* (1991); *Adam* (1992); *Over Forty* (2000). I have written performative essays in popular culture books: Arthur Kroker and Marilousie Kroker (eds), *The Hysterical Male* (Montreal: New World Perspectives, 1991); Shannon Bell, 1995. *Whore Carnival* (New York: Autonomedia, 1995); and Chapter Two of Lisa Johnson (ed.), *Jane Sexes It Up: True Confessions of Feminist Desire* (New York: Seal Press, 2002); "The Female Phallus: Something to See" in Shannon Bell, *Fast Feminism* (New York: Autonomedia, 2010). Deborah Sundahl addressed a number of questions concerning female ejaculation in her advice column "Ask Fanny", which featured in *On Our Backs* throughout the early to mid 1990s. She continues to address female ejaculation questions on her website, www.isismedia.org. In 2003, Sundahl wrote *Female Ejaculation and the G-Spot* (Alameda, CA: Hunter House Inc.); the classic text on female ejaculation. It is a beautiful mesh of female ejaculation knowledge combined with a practical approach to disseminating the skills of female ejaculation, including excellent instructions both for the ejaculator and her partners. It also has an extensive, up-to-date database of research documenting practically everything ever produced on female ejaculation. Furthermore, it is written by a woman who has over twenty years of practical experience teaching other women how to female ejaculate.

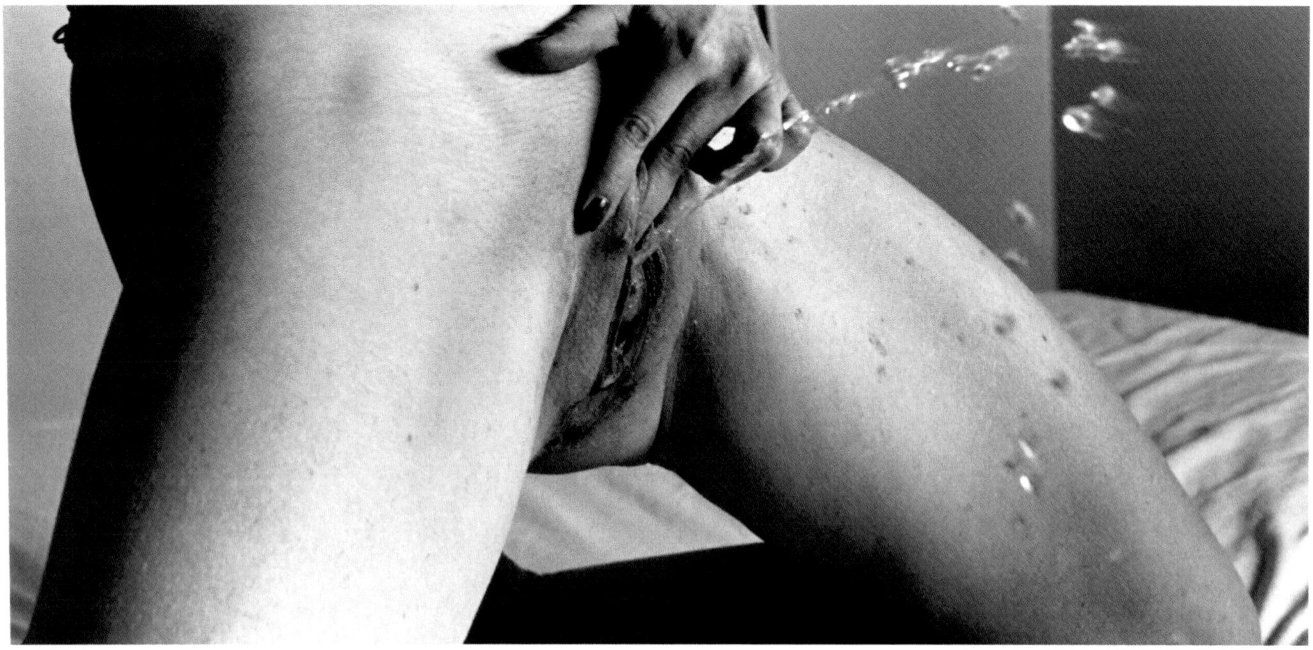

Works Cited

Aristotle (1912). *The Complete Works of Aristotle*. Translated from Greek by A. Platt. Eds J.A. Smith and W.D. Ross. Oxford: Clarendon Press.

Badiou, A (2005) *Being and Event*. Translated from the French by O. Feltham. London: Continuum.

Badiou, A (2001) *Ethics. An Essay on the Understanding of Evil* translated from the French by P. Hallward. London: Verso.

Badiou, A (2002) "On the Truth-process," An Open Lecture by Alain Badiou. The European Graduate School, August. http://www.egs.edu/faculty/alain-badiou/articles/on-the-truth-process/ accessed 01 March 2014.

Badiou, A (2003) *Saint Paul. The Foundation of Universalism*. Trans. R. Brassier. Stanford: Stanford University Press.

Bell, S (2010) *Fast Feminism*. New York: Autonomedia.

Bell, S (1989) Q: What Shoots and Sprays, Shoots and Sprays, Shoots and Sprays? A: A Woman. *Rites* 5(9), p.11.

Bell, S (1995) *Whore Carnival*. New York: Autonomedia.

Boyon, G., and Hanotaux, S (2011) *G Spotting: A Story of Pleasure and Promise* [Documentary] Canada and France: Zadig Productions.

Chalker, R (2000) *The Clitoral Truth: The Secret World at Your Fingertips*. New York: Seven Stories Press.

Chorier, N (1660) 'An Excerpt from a Dialogue between a Married Lady and a Maid' In D. Franich and G. Weatherly eds, (2009) *McSweeney's: Vikings, Monks, Philosopher, Whores Old Forms, Unearthed* 31.

Ellis, H (1936) *Studies in the Psychology of Sex*, Volume II. New York: Random House.

Federation of Feminist Women's Health Centers (1991). *A New View of a Woman's Body*, Los Angeles: Feminist Health Press.

Foucault, M (1990) *History of Sexuality. Volume 1: An Introduction*, trans. Robert Hurley. New York: Vintage Books.

Freud, S [1905] 'Fragments of an Analysis of a Case of Hysteria', In P. Reiff ed. (1993) *Dora: An Analysis of a Case of Hysteria*. New York: Collier Books.

de Graaf, R (1672) *New Treatise Concerning the Generative Organs of Women*. Trans. H. B. Jocelyn and B. P. Setchell (1972) *Journal of Reproduction and Fertility Supplements* 17.

Gräfenberg, E (1950) 'The Role of the Urethra in Female Orgasm', *International Journal of Sexology* 3, pp.145–8.

Ideas: One Sex or Two? Female Ejaculation. CBC Radio, 15 February 1995.

International Documentary Film Festival Amsterdam, [n.d.]. *G Spotting: A Story of Pleasure and Promise*. [Online] Available at: <http://

www.idfa.nl/industry/tags/project.aspx?id=3D4BB728-E2CF-429D-9325-8F3EDFF5A06E> [Accessed 25 August 2013].
Kink.com, (2009) *Squirt Olympics Flower Tucci, Sindee Jennings and Rookie Vai.* [Online] (21 January). Available at: <http://www.fuckingmachines.com/site/shoot/6039-SQUIRT-OLYMPICS-Flower-Tucci-Sindee-Jennings-and-rookie-Vai.html> [accessed 25 August 2013].
Kink.com, (2013) *FuckingMachines.com.* [Online] Available at: <http://www.fuckingmachines.com/> [accessed 25 August 2013].
Krafft-Ebing, R. v. (1965) *Psychopathia Sexualis.* Trans. F. S. Klaf. New York: Stein and Day.
Kroker, A., and Kroker, M. eds, (1991) *The Hysterical Male: New Feminist Theory.* Houndsmill: Macmillan.
Ladas, A., Whipple, B. and Perry, J (1982) *The G-Spot.* New York: Dell Books.
Laqueur, T (1990) *Making Sex: Body and Gender from the Greeks to Freud.* Cambridge, MA: Harvard University Press.
MacKinnon, C (1987) *Feminism Unmodified.* Cambridge, MA: Harvard University Press.
MacKinnon, C (1989) *Toward a Feminist Theory of the State,* Cambridge, MA: Harvard University Press.
Marcus, S (1966) *The Other Victorians: A Study of Sexuality and Pornography in Mid-Nineteenth Century England,* New York: Basic Books.
Plummer, K (1995) *Telling Sexual Stories,* London: Routledge.
Rancière, J (2010) *Dissensus: On Politics and Aesthetics,* translated from the French by S. Corcoran. London: Continuum.
Sherfey, M. J (1972) *The Nature and Evolution of Female Sexuality,* New York: Random House.
Sevely, J. L. and Bennett, J. W (1978) Concerning Female Ejaculation and the Female Prostate, *Journal of Sex Research* 14, pp. 1–20.
Sevely, J. L (1987) *Eve's Secrets: A New Theory of Female Sexuality,* New York: Random House.
Zaviacic, M (1999) *The Human Female Prostate: From Vestigial Skene's Paraurethral Glands and Ducts to Woman's Functioning Prostate,* Bratislava: Slovak Academic Press.

Two's Company, One's a Crowd

Adrian Rifkin

I was wandering, lonely enough, in search of a quotation of which I could hardly trace the source, in notes, in files, no trace, I thought it was to hand, so first thing last, of course, I found it on the internet: it was, as it happened, something I had written, I myself, or rather used, alone, once before, at this computer. Above it were two incipits which, now, I want to use again, because they do put me in mind of this essay, as well as setting up what I had already, once, written. Here they are. I am dropping the authors as these are just isolated, lonely memories of me, that came to me via the internet.

Who am I? I had asked. / Who am I? I replied. / Repetition is, in its difference, accomplishment.

And

There is no speech without response, even if it meets only silence, provided there is someone to hear it.

When I watch jack-off videos on gay sites on the internet, and, indeed, I often do, they offer something of the comfort of the thoroughly indeterminate, the indeterminacy of the enunciation, or the signifier as such, a crowd of lovely daffodils, the rippling field of near identical singularities, near identical in this way or that, an identity itself indeterminable other than the endless shadings of small and greater differences. The truth of the matter is that I find them, on the whole, quite tedious and sometimes unwatchable. On anything longer that 14 seconds, I tend to skip a bit, to jump and see what happens at the end. On the truly long ones, sometimes as much as a quarter of an hour, those of the expert edgers who know how to delay the moment, and, even then, when it comes, to prolong it, I might become so riven in my attention, that the minutes pass quicker than mere seconds.

Not unlike a standard TV thriller, the end is always and already known, and suspense lies not in the narrative itself, but rather in its details, the outcome of the very next 'frame' or edit; with the author, the quality of the scenario, so as to speak. What can he wring out of himself, and what will it signify to me, for me, whether it is much or little, protracted or instantaneous, shot into the air, across a coffee table, staining a settee, against a mirror or even, oh dread, onto the camera lens itself? For me, that is, in my singularity, the absolute particularity in the probable crowd of other viewers; crowds, readers, viewers, daffodils, clouds, cumshots; can I hold on to that, you see, it's just to do with that, that holding on perhaps is, as such, solitary, though whether in its success or relinquishment, I might find it hard to say.

At the same time, it is not unlike the self-conversational landscape of one of those highly educated women of Barbara Pym's novels who, more or less alone in their middle age, turn their thoughts around such issues as these: will the new curate enjoy boiled chicken? What can it mean to and for her if the archdeacon tells her that one of her circle has knitted him socks a little 'short in the feet...?' What precisely, at each moment of its possible recurrence, is the nature of the 'need' for a cup of tea? The instances multiply to become the body of one novel, or a dozen novels, of a whole oeuvre. Reading these novels on the Overground I feel no readier to concede my laughter to a neighbour than I do to show them a video, even a few seconds of some gasping and immense sublimity. That is to say the episteme of what we might call a collectivity of monads, or of a certain loneliness in the frame of a repetitive sociability already and, perhaps, always analogically links the most improbable comparatives.

In any event I had thought to valorise these lost and lonely hours like this. I was to make an art video installation of some kind. I had noticed, quite early on in my years of viewing, that the point where these videos take off is, queerly enough, at their very end: the moment when the actions of the hand, the squelching and so forth are sublimated in a groan, a series of grunts when another singularity emerges, the grain of a body that is in the throat. It was enough that I was, am here to hear it. So the project was and remains this: that I would, and perhaps will, take the best downloads from my collection and swiftly edit them so that however long or short, and on the simplest of algorithms, they would play over and over until, finally, before the loops begin again, they all groan together. These videos should play with the image too dark to see and the sound turned up to the point of absolute displeasure. Hard to measure, but at least my two old incipits would be once again fulfilled in solitude's own, final, crowded shot.

Conception

Antony Gormley

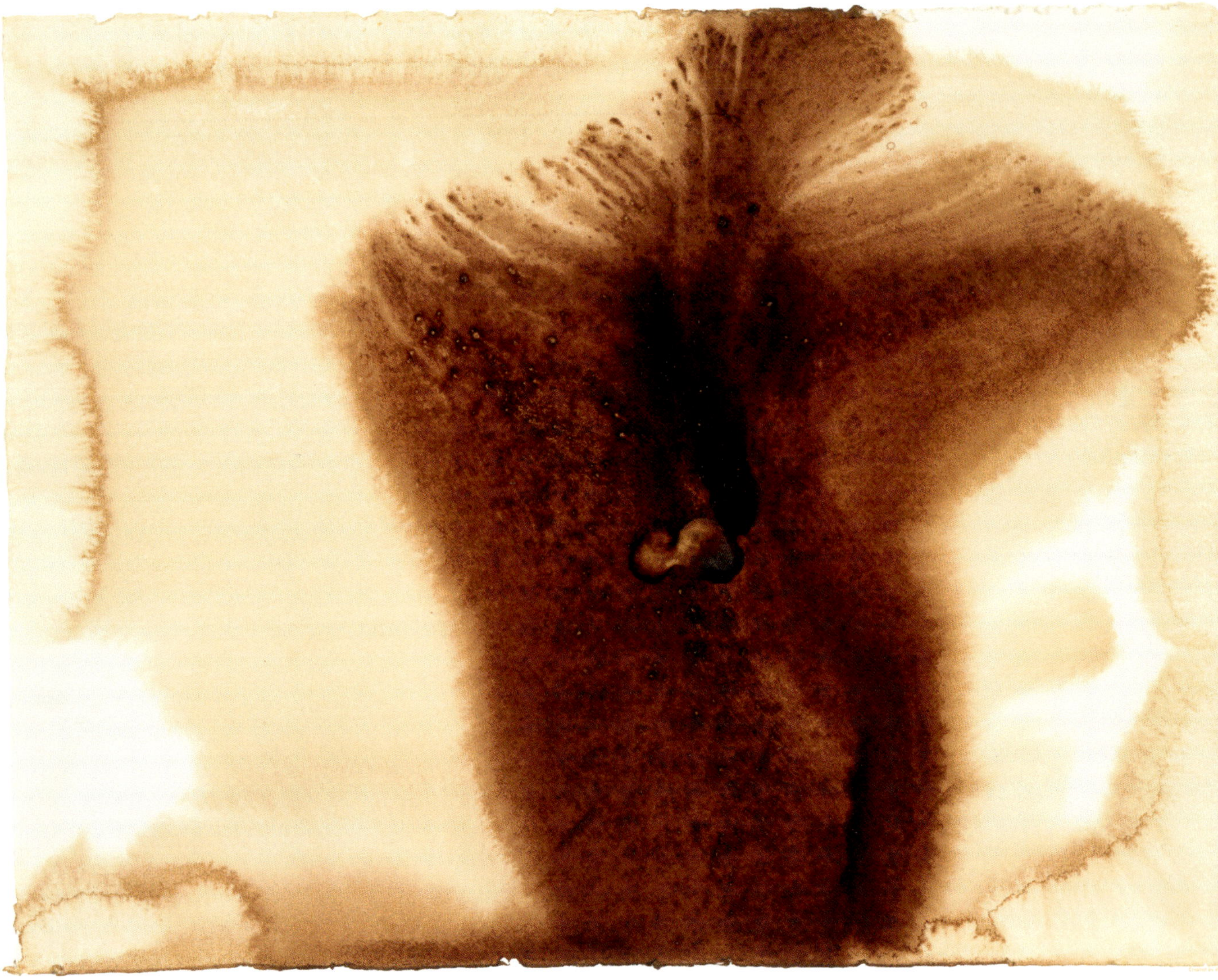

Spent

Jordan McKenzie

A true, all RAW, DADDY BEAR, GANG BANG FUCK FEST! COCKED AND LOADED features 7 hot Daddies fucking 1 lucky bottom boy… a total cast of 8 ass ploughing, cum eating studs, fucking non-stop for 80 minutes all for your pleasure… COCKED AND LOADED features real man to man ass banging… with some of the most awesome feltching scenes you will ever see. And, of course, all the trademark close-up shots by the legendary Michael McKey as he zooms in so you get to see every drop of cum and every man-ramming minute.

8.01. That's what it says on the porn star's watch as he begins his ecstatic, over-acted climax. I can see it clearly on the screen, a silver digital watch with a grey face and black LED numbering. The counter on the silver DVD recorder shows me that I am 28 minutes and 39 seconds into the 'fuck fest'. The clock on my mobile telephone lying next to the bright orange sheet of universal litmus paper shows me that it is 10.30 exactly. A triangular interface of three separate moments all 'shot' through by a porn stars' orgasm. Maybe there is another kind of a clock in the room, the fingers of my hand wrapped around my dick, a five-digit flesh metronome, each stroke of my hand keeping time, the rhythm see-sawing, faster and slower, creating a score of the fizzing pressure of my own orgasm, getting nearer, ebbing away, getting nearer again, as my hand strokes and hesitates, strokes and hesitates.

The DVD's that I have been watching are getting progressively more explicit, no frills, no music, no soft lighting just hard, super-sharp fucking. I have produced over one hundred and fifty semen drawings. I described them once as a mapping of desire for an exhibition catalogue. I was wrong. They don't map desire; they map mechanical reproduction, repeatability, and the boredom of making over and over again. The material evidence of these drawings reduces my orgasm to a mere methodology, an A to a B. My need for explicit images is a need to get it over with, to make the composition, make it number one hundred and fifty one. It is not porn that is brutalising me but drawing, the voluntary act of turning my body into a system, a sequential unit of pictorial production.

My experience is fractured, not the self-absorbed onanistic pleasure of libidinal need but an array of necessities that disperse the encounter with myself. Propped up awkwardly on a cushion leaning on my left arm, remote control in hand. The litmus paper in front of my cock angled slightly up to the left so that the 'composition' can be framed on the paper. My eyes shift from screen, to remote, to paper... back to screen. The rhythm of intercourse on the screen falls into the rhythm of my hand and then my hand falls behind, the endless edited thrusting explored from every angle, known visually from all sides. The ache in my left arm reminds me that it needs to move; I angle my body closer to the paper.

The porn stars eyes have betrayed him. As he waited his turn at the 'cum hole' his eyes flicked towards the camera. I am no longer the eternal voyeur visually eves-dropping, the straight trajectory of his desire has been disrupted and he has acknowledged his performance within the scene no matter how quickly he takes his eyes away again. The remote, the paper, frame my own scene, puncturing the smooth flow of my own desire. The shadow of a boom mike crosses his leg and then quickly withdraws, as he steps towards the bed he reveals a clothed boy behind him sitting on a sofa. How old is he? Early to middle twenties? He is wearing a grey t-shirt and blue jeans, a clipboard clutched to his chest with campy efficiency. His gaze is not boredom, or invested physical interest, but a kind of efficient directorial stare at a job getting done. I too have bodies to direct, and paper, an orange screen for my efficient ejaculations, director and performer, a producer and consumer. My arm begins to hurt, time to shift again, angling my body further from the paper this time.

Fast forward, rewind, trying to get just the right moment. I can digitally control these porn stars, get them to re-enter or cum again and again endlessly repeating their contorted faces at the moment of orgasm, finding my favourite position, my eyes eating the screen. Click, not close enough, click, not extreme enough, always trying to see more, to catch every texture of the skin of the cock, to scoop up the last visual viscosity of the semen as it spatters onto the face and chest of the 'bottom'.

I am never in it. No imagined positions or transference, no attempt to be a top or bottom my eyeballs are dispassionate and disconnected to the rest of my body but slip over not into the screen. I can feel my balls beginning to tighten, here is the familiar conclusion, not eagerly anticipated but not necessarily uninvited either. End of the process. I move my hand quickly up and down my cock, the rhythm quickening pace with the porn star so that we can come together. He is purely focused on the money shot, isolated in his own universe and strangely separate from the bottom who watches with a staged anticipation but also with a kind of locked out distanced look on his face.

If I am so separate from the screen then why do I 'cum' with him? Why do I want to perform this sexual swoon at exactly the same time? Am I slipping into the directed fantasy of the film, are the cries of 'yes, yes cum, shoot it' for me? To me? Of me?

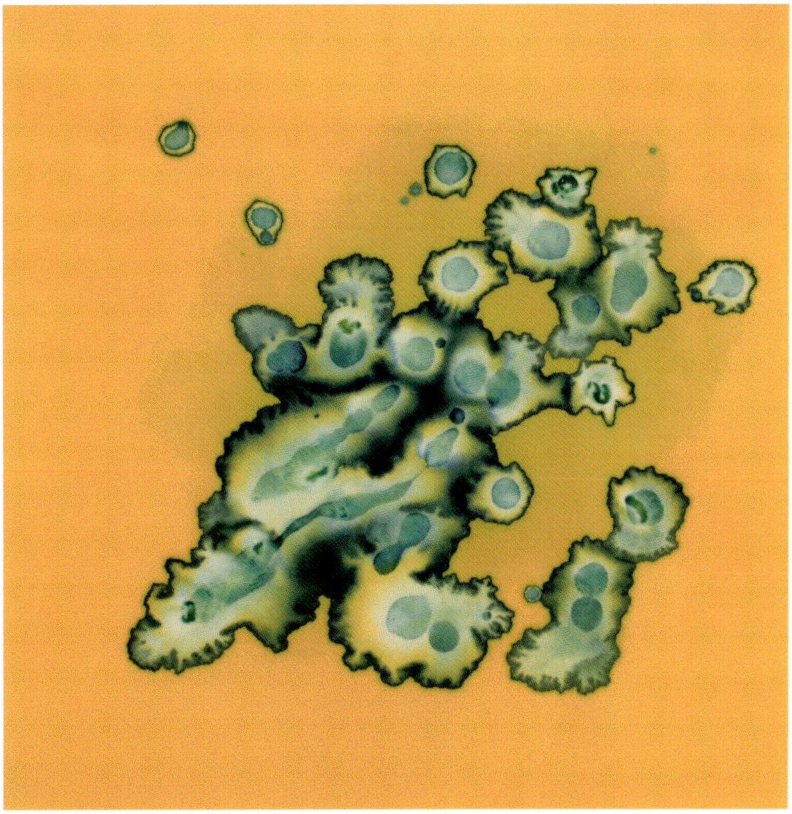

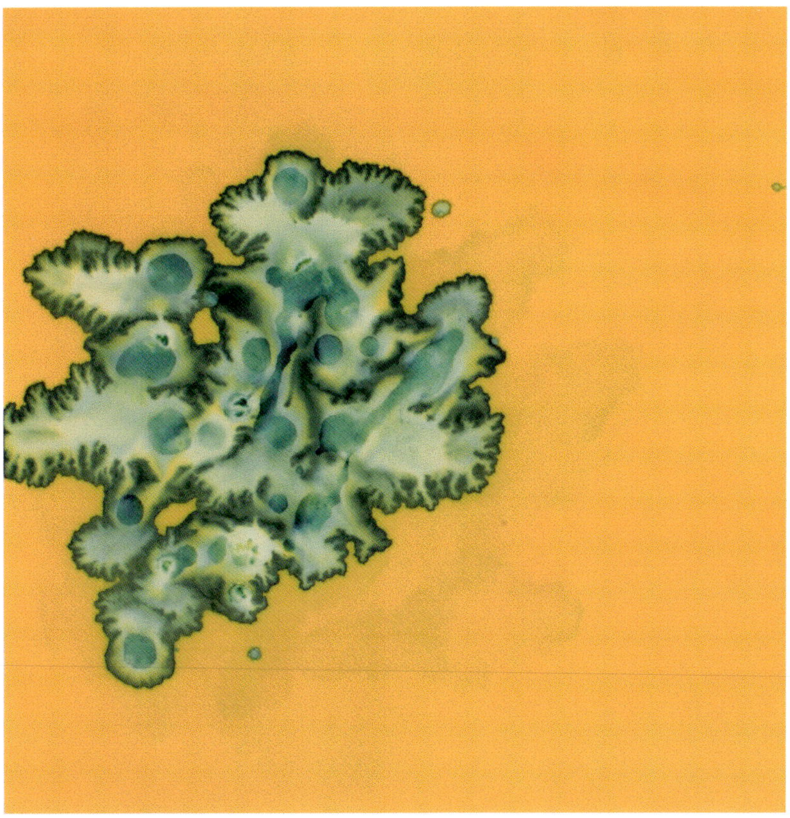

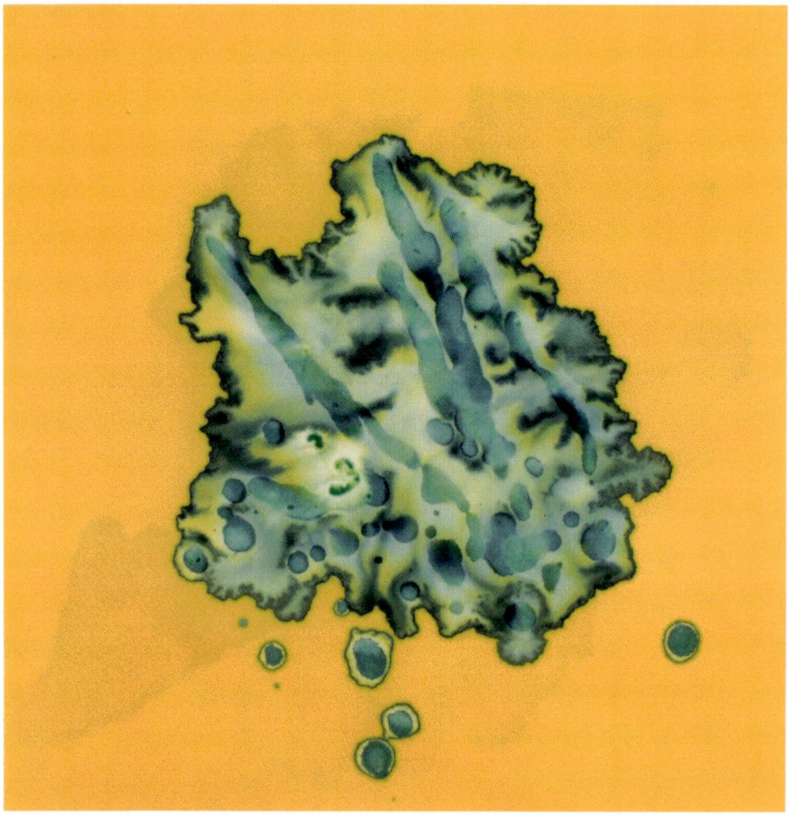

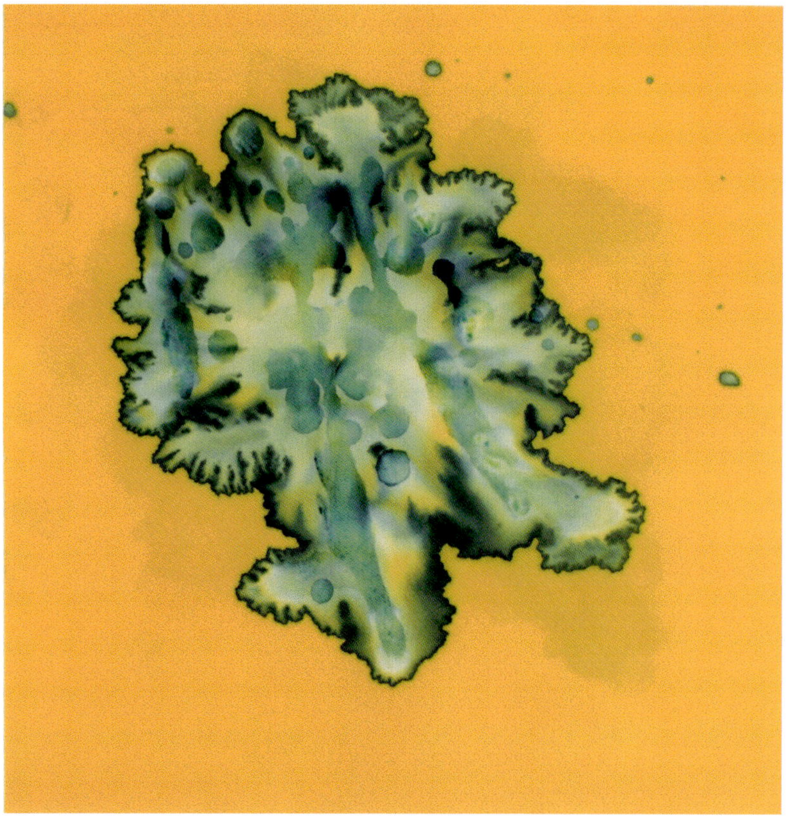

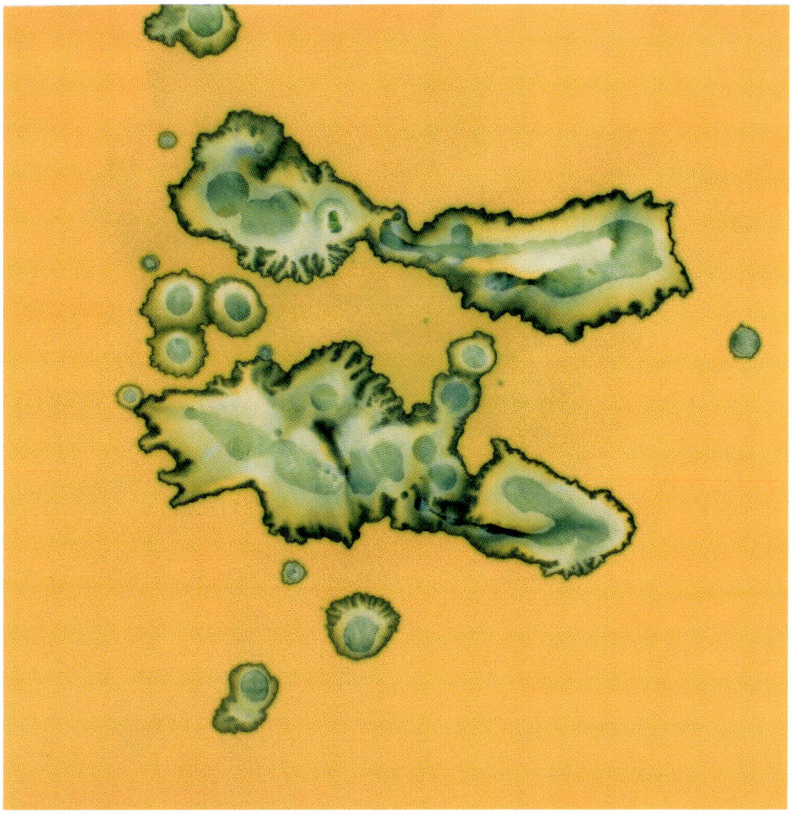

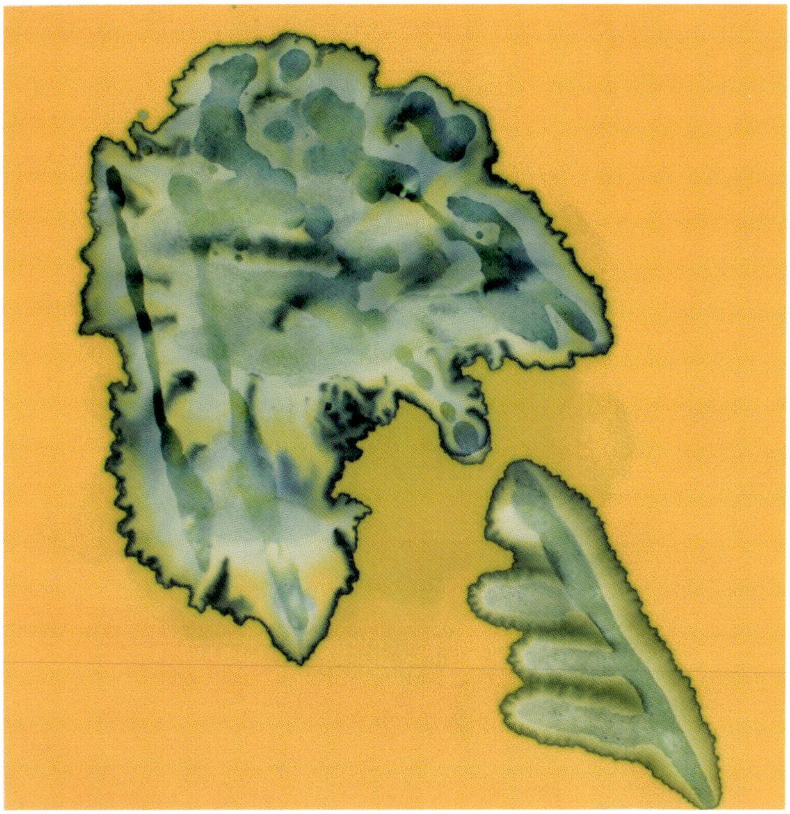

In-take of breath... eyes too wide to see and then the charges through my body and the separate thrusts of my balls as the semen is pushed out of my dick. I am not lost in the drenched feeling of orgasm, never un-tethered or oblivious as my eyes quickly dart downwards across my chest and down onto my penis. This is my money shot, making sure the semen hits the orange of the paper, the litmus target. I try not to compose, not to frame the orgasm but, as the now dead, meaningless and hollow sounds of the porn movie continue on with its 'fuck-fest', I move my cock around so that it creates flicks and splashes, an onanistic Pollock tracing loops. As soon as the semen hits the litmus paper it turns green, no longer anything to do with me, that green is the shut off, the severing away from myself. That green is the objective, dispassionate evidence, an aesthetic mould that bleeds away from the private, the inside and onto the public.

Press the **Off** button.

Cum time: 10.56
Cum Date: 06/08/08

Circlejerker

Dominic Johnson

The act of creative self-representation will always run the risk of being received as narcissistic, masturbatory, or navel-gazing. In performance art, where the body of the artist becomes or tends to be conflated with the field or object of representation, and where abstractions and distractions may melt away to present the body of the artist as apparently unmediated, the risk of total exposure is accentuated to the point of humiliation. With watching performance comes the threat of identifying too strongly with the object of one's perception: in wanting *to become* or *to be with* the body one attends to (a confusion fundamental to object-choice) the viewing subject encounters publicly the critical embarrassment of indulging one's own pleasures, of making a spectacle of one's unspoken wants or refusals, and the shame of naysaying the scene of one's desiring investments.

In his collected essays, *Rarely Pure and Never Simple*, the cultural critic and pornographer Scott O'Hara writes, 'There is a popular notion that "Pleasure shared is pleasure doubled". I think this cliché was thought up by repressed Puritans who were afraid of the idea of solitary pleasure'.(1) A writer, performer, publisher and 'pleasure activist', O'Hara is perhaps remembered best for the rare ability to hold his cock in his own mouth. The act impressed audiences in live performances from his debut in 1983, and earned him the mock-official title of 'The Biggest Dick in San Francisco'.(2) He was a candid and provocative writer, who published two collections of essays, and edited the journal *Steam* (subtitled 'the literate queer's guide to sex and controversy'). He died of AIDS in 1998, at the age of 37.

In his essay 'Do It Yourself', O'Hara describes his now-legendary jack-off shows of the early 1980s. Taking to the stage, he would parade his costume – military, cowboy, leather – and then slowly strip down to a jockstrap. 'That gave me a chance to strut around a little more, show off some more, show them my butthole'. In the text, his audience is a regimented mass of seething desire, 'one man, a man with fifty dicks, all being beaten off at the same time'. Twenty minutes into his live show, he would pull off his jockstrap and drape it round his neck, to chew on intermittently through the remaining half of the performance.'

> All I had to do was look at my shadow on the movie screen behind me, the silhouette of my dick sticking out in front of me, larger than life, then poke a finger or two into my asshole - and I'd go into a frenzy [...] my hands [w]ould wander my body, fingers exploring

my ass or pinching my tits or spreading my buttcheeks for eager voyeurs, or rubbing my armpits and then sucking the sweat off.

His tumescence now a perfect upward arc, O'Hara would limber up for the showstopper: placing his hands on his buttocks while in a standing position, he would lower his head and grip his penis between his lips, before the gasps and whoops of the man with fifty cocks. Swaggering round the stage soon after, O'Hara would position himself in profile, 'sneering in friendly fashion at those men who I had in the palm of my hand' (along, that is, with his famous member), and release a prodigious stream of ejaculate, its silver trails picked out in airborne sparkles by the light, and shadowed in grey on the white projector screen. 'That's when I'd stare out at him and smile, as I licked the cum off my hand, making it real clear how much I loved eating my own cum. No acting required. Then I'd gather up the rest of my clothes, [and] take a bow – grinning, exhausted, but happy'.(3)

I claim O'Hara's autofellatio – and more generally the cultural logic of solitary pleasure – towards an assertion of the critical urgency of narcissism (as a speaking *to* and *from* a coincidence of positions and pleasures), a coming full-circle of the masturbatory endeavour. If autofellatio stages the explicit culmination of the gesture of navel-gazing, the act is troubled by its status as performance: it is conflicted in its self-pleasuring introversion by being directed outwards towards an audience. Looking for a politics of solitary pleasure, and towards the celebration of queer, inward-looking histories of performance art, I read O'Hara's public attempts at self-incorporation through the mystical and alchemical archetype of the ouroboros, or self-eating serpent. For Silviano Santiago, the ouroboros is a sign for meta-discourse, whereby the emblem's co-signification of 'aggression' and narcissistic 'complacency' figures the state of any theory as caught between progressive politics and methodological dogmatism.(4) For John Visvader, 'uroboric philosophies' are any programmes of thought that bear 'the peculiar characteristic of having as one of its goals its own demise'. 'Self-referential' and narcissistic, these philosophies proceed via what he terms a 'dialectics of self-erasure'.(5)

O'Hara's recollections of his sexual adventures, as a bathhouse queen and public sex devotee, and not least his accounts of sex shows, are striking for their persistent narration of an apparently perfect narcissism. His descriptions are coloured by a heightened sense of erotic self-sufficiency, loaded with a desperate dependency upon the responsive adulation of his audience. He took intense pleasures in performance, an erotic indulgence that is clearly redoubled in his re-writing of these scenes. Yet such vigorous romance slips neatly into disaster. 'The fantasies I had', he writes, 'of that fifty-cocked man coming on stage and raping me with every one of his cocks', urged on in his public pleasures towards a fantasy of serial violation.

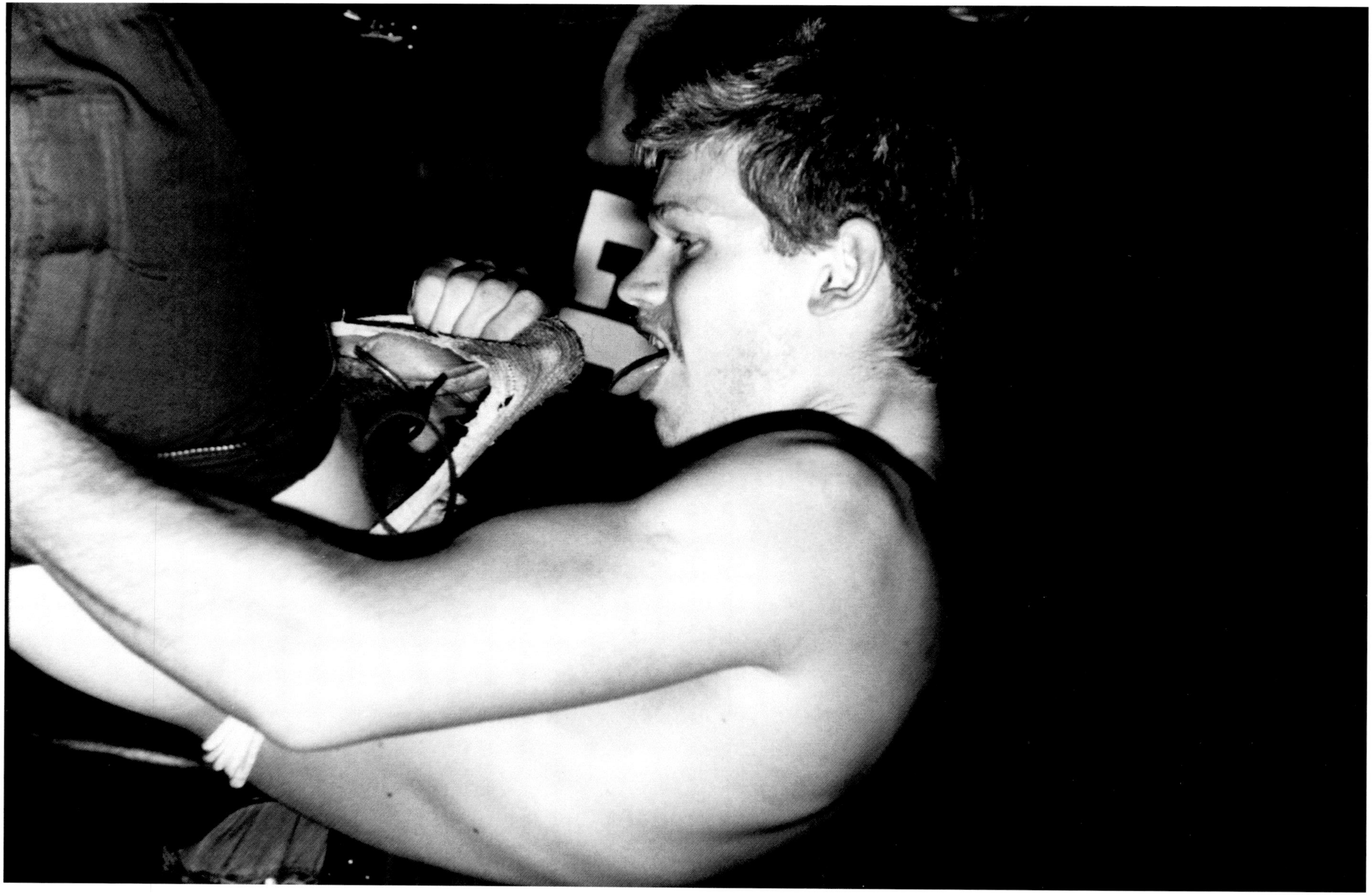

***Scott O'Hara in the Powerhouse Greasy Jockstrap Contest, San Francisco* (1985)** Robert Pruzan

O'Hara's pleasurable self-incorporations in performance, twice nightly, three times a week, throughout the 1980s, secure his place alongside an esoteric lineage of artists who have similarly represented the act of autofellatio in their work. John Cameron Mitchell's film *Shortbus* (2006) is a recent and mainstream manifestation, where the act is a metonymic signifier for the film's introspective, romantically blocked, suicidal artist-protagonist. The self-suck is in fact a recurrent trope in the history of art, especially in photographic auto-portraiture. An early pioneer of this obscure pedigree is Pierre Molinier, who at 72 built an apparatus to enable his aging frame to redouble on itself in autofellatio, as recorded in an autoportrait in the early 1970s; a direct inheritor of Molinier's tortured design, Ron Athey's *Solar Anus* (2000) upends the logic of autofellatio with an auto-penetrative cancan, probing his own rectum with his high-heels' phallic protuberances. In a photograph from his *Dream Days* series of 2002, Matthias Herrmann licks the tip of his own cock; the white expanse of a radiator echoes the movie screen in O'Hara's performance, framing, it would seem, the centrality of projection and representation in the art of autofellatio. A gestures towards autofellatio appears promiscuously in Peter Hujar's libidinally charged portrait, *Daniel Schook Sucking Toe* (1981): a lithe young man with a bowl haircut props one crossed leg upon the other to grasp his big toe in his mouth, gazing with a kind of lugubrious dignity at the camera while a lazy arm hangs heavy down the frame.

The symbolic power of autofellatio borrows from the cultural politics of both oral sex and masturbation in the twentieth century. In an odd monograph on the former, Leo Abse argues, 'fellatio cannot be treated as a political irrelevance'.(6) Two of the most newsworthy celebrity scandals of the 1990s – concerning illicit blowjobs received by Bill Clinton and Hugh Grant – owed at least part of their notoriety to the non-reproductive sex act's curious cultural weight. In his lucid critical history of masturbation, Thomas Lacqueur argues that its solitary pleasures call into question the individual's relation to society, highlighting the ethical, moral, and political ramifications that attend to socialisation. After the 'invention' of modern masturbation in the eighteenth century, the autonomous practitioner, for Lacqueur, defines her or his pleasures in terms of discipline, self-determination, secrecy, guilt, and the measure of excess. In the Freudian paradigm, masturbation is a phase through which the subject must pass in order to attain adult sexuality (Krafft-Ebing's case studies in *Psychopathia Sexualis* demonstrate the apparently grave implications for those in whom this passage fails). Whereas masturbation may signify independency, self-sufficiency and imagination, in the wrong hands, it implies self-indulgence, solipsism, and stalled adolescence. Owing to the contradiction between the logics of moralism and sexual liberation, masturbation became, in Lacqueur's words, 'a practice of individual autonomy and of sexual energy, an instrument of freedom, or, in the minds of some, a sign of abjection and despair. Self-pleasuring teeters between utopia and its opposite'.(7)

To return explicitly to self-sucking, its specialisation as a masturbatory endeavour has earned close study in the annals of clinical psychiatry, where it is referred to variously as 'autofellatio', 'self-fellatio', or the less common 'self-irrumation'.(8) In a 1977 article in the *Journal of Nervous and Mental Disease*, three psychiatrists provide a clinical survey of autofellators, following Alfred Kinsey's (obviously conservative) estimate that 'the incidence of autofellatio or autofellatio fantasies may be as high as two or three out of 1000 men'.(9) Their case studies include a homosexual who learned the act after watching contortionists at a circus; two military men and two sons of long-distance truck drivers; a further case, suspiciously, 'had long curls till age 4 and was never allowed to play with boys', and, suffice to say, 'his mother was the dominant parent' (Cavenar, p. 359). Another's commitment to autofellatio was accompanied by a dizzying list of 'perversions', including 'pedophilia, cunnilinguism, homosexuality, exhibitionism, transvestism, fetishism, algol[a]gnia [or sadomasochism], and voyeurism'. This latter autofellator preferred to 'perform for an observer [and] obtained more pleasure when the observer was shocked'. The psychiatrists read his symptoms as pathological manifestations of 'a fantasy of self-impregnation; he felt that a self-induced pregnancy would make him special and provide enjoyment', recalling perhaps the messianic fantasies recounted in the memoirs of Daniel Paul Schreber. Throughout the eight case studies reported by Cavenar et al, the drive to autofellatio is read neatly as a conflict between, on the one hand, 'intense narcissism' and 'underdeveloped object relations' and, on the other, 'extreme' yet compromised dependencies. While it would be easy to critique the study's premises and conclusions, I hazard taking these clinical fantasists at their word. This queer sincerity entails reading the act of autofellatio as staging a symbolic conflict between radical narcissism and a compromised fantasy of relational dependency. As such, we might celebrate O'Hara's creative autofellatio, and affirm it as the unapologetic revelation of the self, its needs and pleasures, at the centre of an unlikely project of critical thought. Doing so describes an urgency that bleeds outwards into partial and inconsolable illuminations of our responsibilities towards and dependencies upon others. 'Little did I know,' O'Hara would write, 'the kind of power bestowed by a mere nine inches of turgid flesh'.(10)

In *Margins of Philosophy*, Derrida reads the scene of writing as a painful 'mirroring' of the self: an act that takes 'just the time to recognize or reflect [the writer] and immediately to turn away.'(11) It is an about-face towards communication that he describes through the furtive figure of Narcissus, with explicit reference to both ouroboros and autofellatio. The crisis of becoming present to oneself through writing is narcissistic and dependent: the writer is 'cut off from the source', but also 'multipled or divided by the difference of the other'. The 'turning away' of the writer to the source and back again is described as the logic of a broken circle: a repetition that cannot return to an origin proper, but rather, as a snake that bites its own tail, one that gives rise to the mythical circuit of the ouroboros; the line turns *upon* itself, 'thereby affecting and infecting itself, [to...] poison the question of meaning' (Derrida, 1982, pp. 277-78). Derrida is wrangling here with the possibility of the 'source' as a theme in the poetry of Paul Valéry, though he turns to the impasse of autobiographical writing, as what he terms a 'compulsive obstinacy' in which the 'source' is the self. Refusing representation, the self 'can never be [...] *posed* before a glance, facing it; it never constitutes a present or hidden unity, an object or a subject [...] whose meanings or substantial content at heart would remain identical to [itself]' (Derrida, 1982, p. 279). The self is that origin against which exteriority appears, and appears to take on meaning. Therefore, 'the I, the exception to and condition for everything that appears, does not appear' (Derrida, 1982, p. 281). Writing, for Derrida 'encircles, or rather tracks down, this incessant disappearance,' a description that might be fittingly extended to the work of performance, whose rhetoric emerges throughout Derrida's essay. 'Incapable of putting itself *onstage*, pure consciousness therefore cannot give itself any image of itself [...] As soon as it *performs* Narcissus's turn, it no longer knows itself' (Derrida, 1982, pp. 284-5, emphases added). This death of self-sameness is therefore the condition for the acknowledgement of others. By depending on communication, narcissism performs itself to others, breaking the closed circuit of self-representation. Amelia Jones concurs when she notes that '[n]arcissism, enacted through body art, turns the subject inexorably and paradoxically outward.'(12)

It is interesting that Derrida describes the breaking open of the internalised event of self-representation as a 'cutting', a harmful separation from the dream of independent self-fulfilment, splintering the fantasy of a purely solitary pleasure. 'The snake bites its tail', he writes, 'from which above all it does not follow that it finally rejoins itself without harm in this successful auto-fellatio of which we have been speaking all along, in truth' (Derrida, 1982, p. 289). The psychiatric reading of autofellatio discussed earlier preempts Derrida's findings via the punitive language of psychosexual pathology: his account of the subject's autobiographical encounter - described elsewhere as 'auto-affection'(13) - parallels Cavenar et al, for whom the autofellator stages a conflict between self-sufficiency and dependency. Writes in his memoir, *Autopornography*, O'Hara bursts the bubble of autofellatio, and of the relationality it might seem merely to pantomime: 'It's painful, and not really that satisfying. Still, it does give me that irreplaceable feeling of having a dick between my lips [...] when there aren't any other options. [...] It's a lot better than having to keep a lover around' (O'Hara, 1997, p. 118). Mimicking Derrida's image, O'Hara stages the crisis of self-presence that arises in an exemption from the properly social relation of love or romance: the priority of self-reliance over dependency is performed as an unstable condition for pleasure, and for knowledge. As the practices of self-representation in art and performance seem to hint at, if the capacity for 'auto-affection' is the condition of experience itself, the spectacle of solitary pleasure may enable the writing of one's own critical and sexual urgencies – without forgetting the needs and social realities of others.

Acknowledgement

Parts of this chapter appear in different forms in Dominic Johnson (2012) 'Ecstatic Intervals: Performance in a Continuum of Intimacy', in *Intimacy: Across Visceral and Digital Performance*, ed. by Maria Chatzichristodoulou and Rachel Zerihan, Houndsmills and New York: Palgrave Macmillan, pp. 89-101.

Endnotes

1.Scott O'Hara (1999) 'Handcuffed Together', *Rarely Pure and Never Simple: Selected Essays of Scott O'Hara*, ed. by Steven Zeeland, New York and London: Harrington Park Press, p. 208.
2. Scott O'Hara (1997) *Autopornography: A Memoir of Life in the Lust Lane*, New York and London: Harrington Park Press, p. 70.
3. O'Hara (1999) 'Do It Yourself', *Rarely Pure and Never Simple: Selected Essays of Scott O'Hara*, ed. by Steven Zeeland, New York and London: Harrington Park Press, pp. 98-101.
4. Silviano Santiago (1971) 'Ouroboros', *MLN* 86.6, December, 790-792, p. 790.
5. John Visvader (1978)'The Use of Paradox in Uroboric Philosophies', *Philosophy East and West* 28.4, October, pp. 455-467, p. 455.
6. Leo Abse (2000) *Fellatio: Masochism, Politics and Love*, London: Robson Books, p. xix.
7. Thomas W. Laqueur (2003) *Solitary Sex: A Cultural History of Masturbation*, New York: Zone Books, p. 22.
8. Eugene Kahn and Ernest G. Lion, (1938) 'A Clinical Note on a Self-Fellator', *American Journal of Psychiatry* 95, July, 131-33, p. 131.
9. Jesse O. Cavenar Jr., Jean G. Spaulding and Nancy T. Butts (1977) 'Autofellatio: A Power and Dependency Conflict', *Journal of Nervous and Mental Disease*, 165.5, November, 356-360, p. 356.
10. O'Hara (1999) 'Learning Lust', *Rarely Pure and Never Simple: Selected Essays of Scott O'Hara*, ed. by Steven Zeeland, New York and London: Harrington Park Press, p. 93.
11. Jacques Derrida (1982) 'Qual Quelle: Valéry's Sources', 1971, *Margins of Philosophy*, trans. by Alan Bass, New York and London: Harvester Wheatsheaf, p. 275.
12. Amelia Jones (1998) *Body Art/Performing the Subject*, Minneapolis: University of Minnesota Press, p. 48.
13. Jacques Derrida (1976) *Of Grammatology*, trans. by Gayatri Chakravorty Spivak, Baltimore and London: Johns Hopkins University Press, p. 165.

We made love with Marcel Duchamp / Ephemera

Beth Stephens & Annie Sprinkle

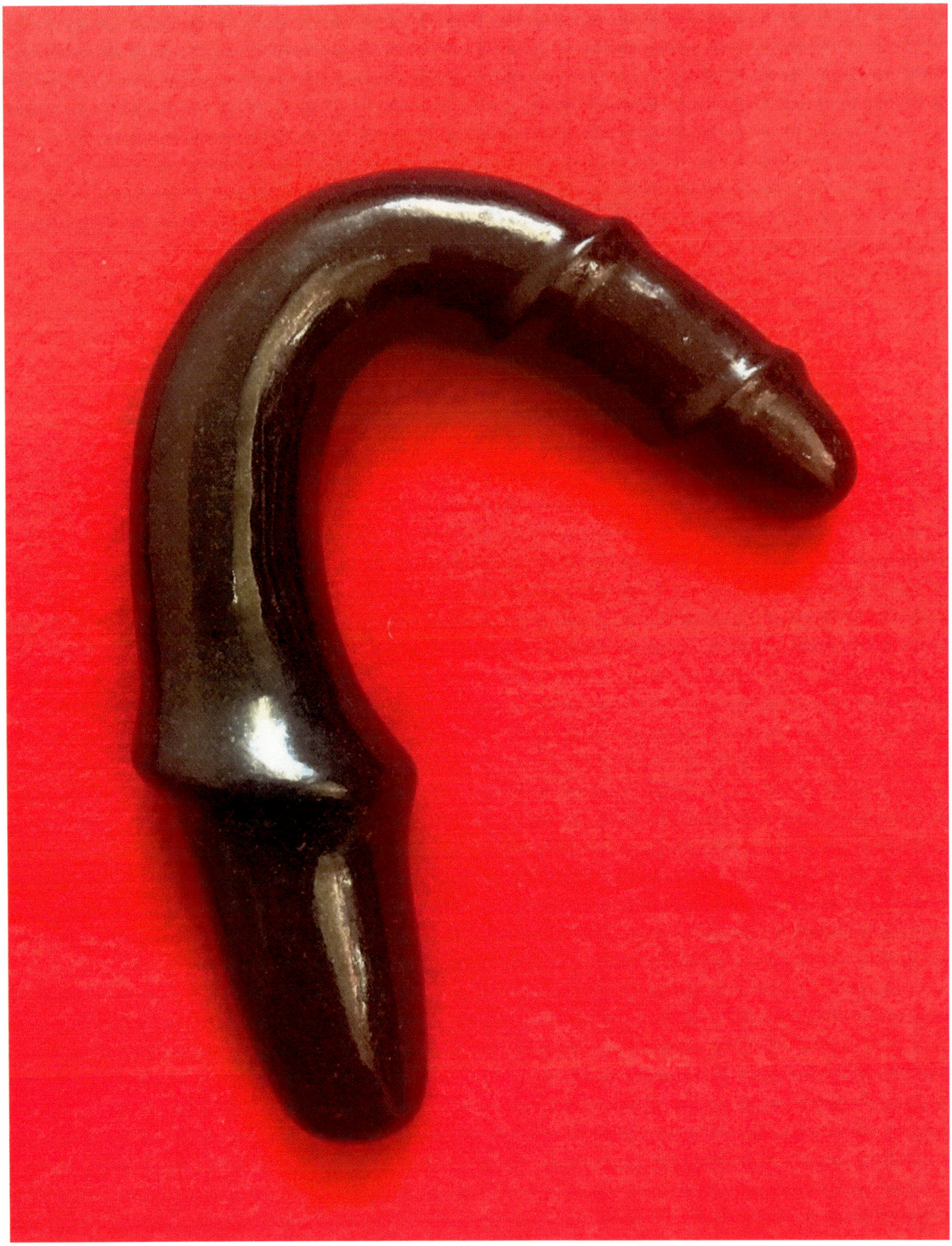

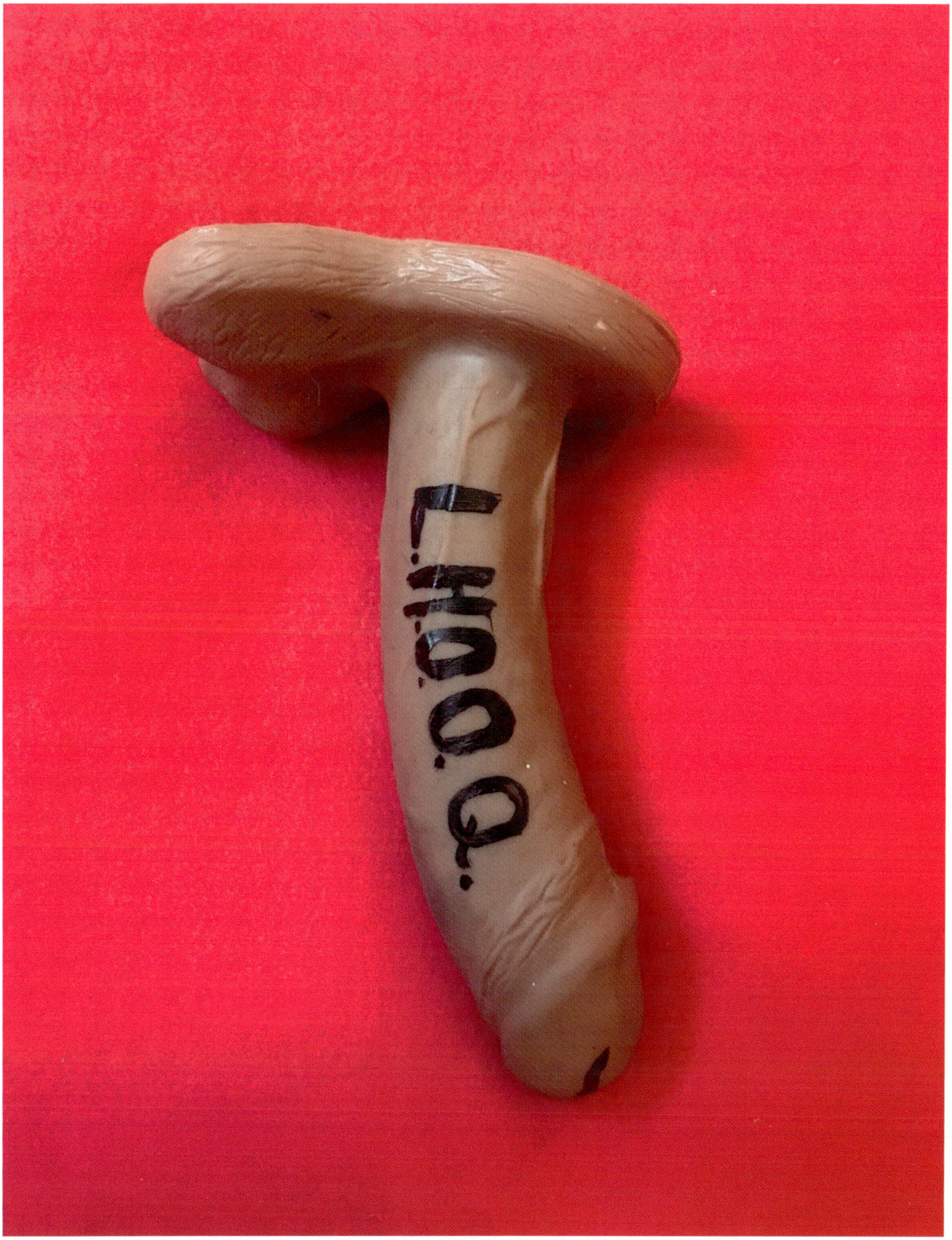
L.H.O.O.Q.

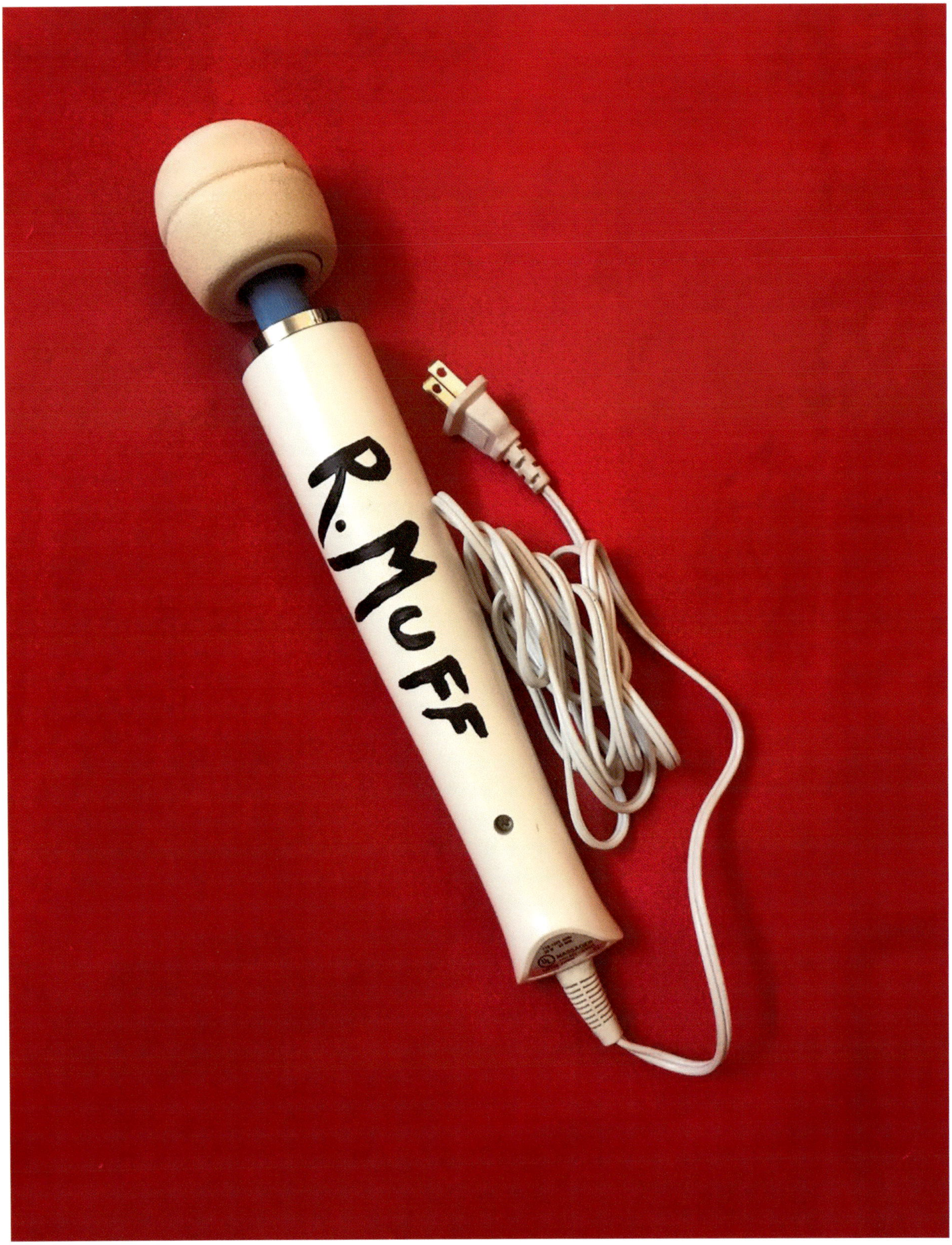
R.MUFF

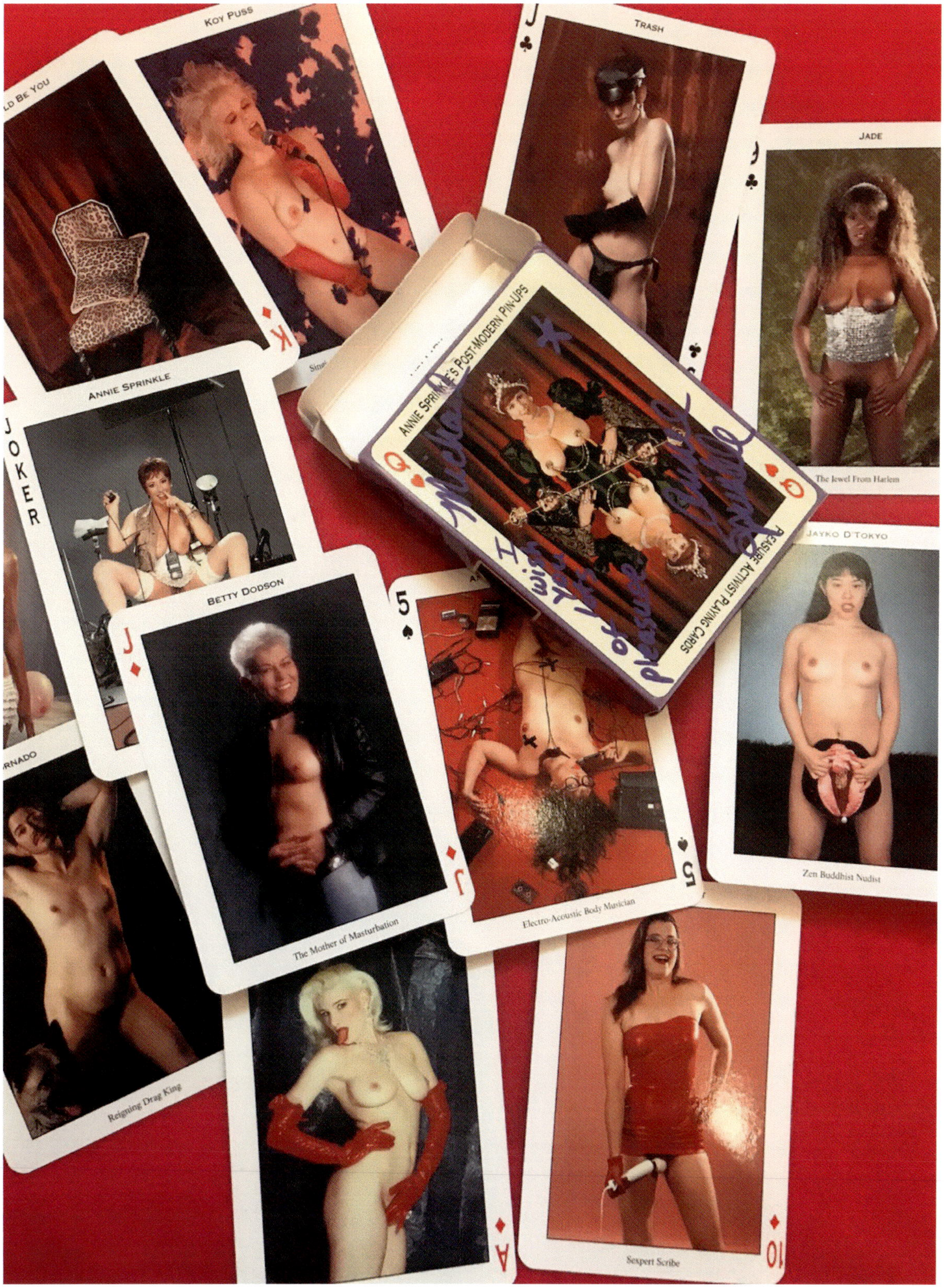
KOY PUSS
TRASH
JADE
The Jewel From Harlem
ANNIE SPRINKLE
JOKER
ANNIE SPRINKLE'S POST-MODERN PIN-UPS
PLEASURE ACTIVIST PLAYING CARDS
JAYKO D'TOKYO
BETTY DODSON
The Mother of Masturbation
Electro-Acoustic Body Musician
Zen Buddhist Nudist
Reigning Drag King
Sexpert Scribe

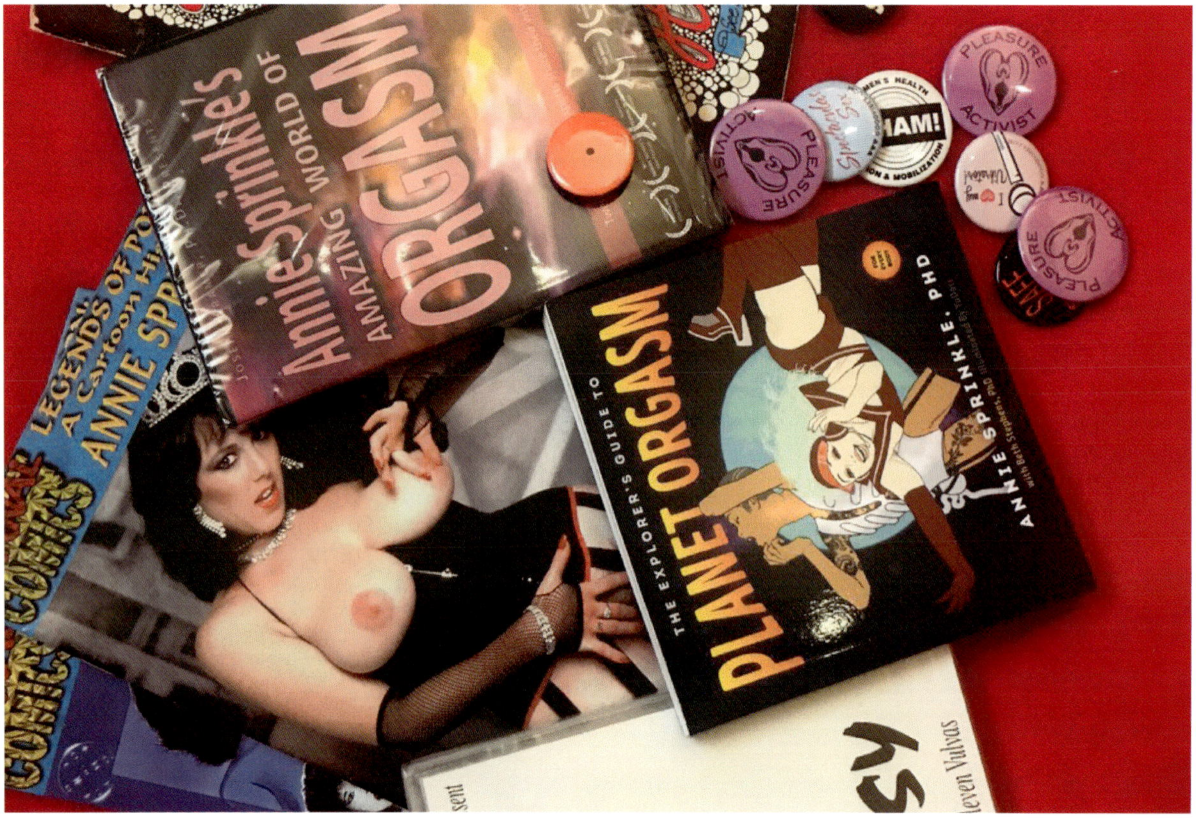
Annie Sprinkle's
AMAZING WORLD OF
ORGASM
THE EXPLORER'S GUIDE TO
PLANET ORGASM
ANNIE SPRINKLE, PHD
PLEASURE ACTIVIST

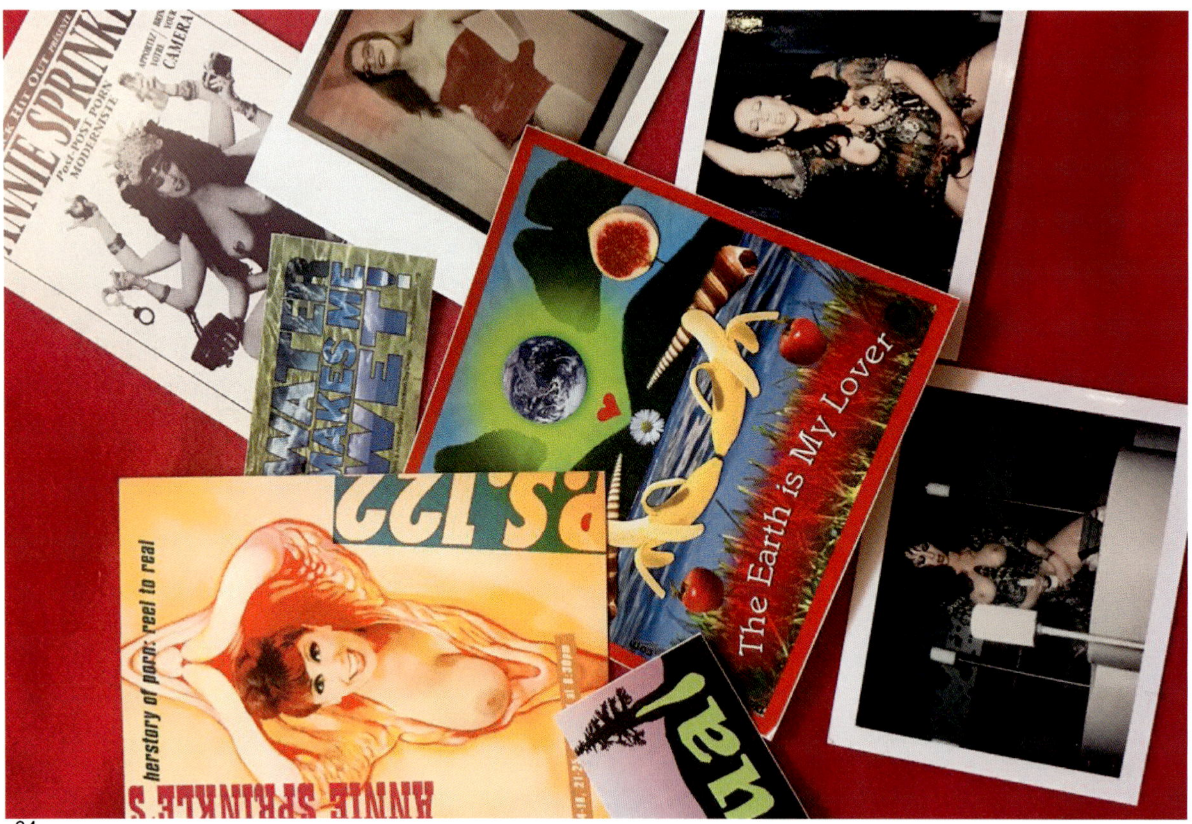
Post-POST PORN MODERNIST
WATER MAKES ME WET!
The Earth is My Lover
P.S.122
ANNIE SPRINKLE'S
herstory of porn: reel to real

Sexual Subjectivity

Susie Orbach

I think sexuality, and sexual response, particularly for women, is very complex, despite all the talk of sex in our culture. Young women are often not clear or comfortable with their own sexual development. They're not being introduced to it very well. They're told how to put condoms on, rather than introduced to their clitoris and yet they see soft porn of women being desired and apparently desiring in images incessantly. Brought up to be there for others they can be too shy or unwilling to be there for themselves. Learning about their own bodies is vital. *You're the only one who can learn it*, so to speak.

If people don't know their own sexual response at a minimal level when they come to be with others, they're in difficulty. So I'm not sure I think masturbation is important because it's the great solitary pleasure, but rather because it's a gateway into understanding aspects of your body and your delight and the pleasure you can experience. Such understanding may, then, allow you to connect with others, without feeling left out or exploited or whatever.

Adolescents and teenagers need to develop a sense of themselves as sexual beings that's focused on them, that's self-reflexive, and affirmative, all the more so in this #metoo moment, which is both disturbing and a real chance to harness a certain affirmative power.

In this broad context, psychoanalysis and psychology are useful because they understand very well what happens when things go wrong for people. When people aren't able to find a sexual subjectivity, they have alienating forms of trying to connect both to themselves and others. It's important to see what happens when people aren't able to find their sexual selves; that's part of what psychoanalysis looks at. I don't think masturbation raises anything particularly critical for psychoanalysis, and while there's loads of stuff on the topic in Freud, that's not what interests me. What's important is that sexual subjectivity is understood as a part of self, and, if it isn't met, then there are ways in which one dies inside. Psychoanalysis becomes a way of helping people both *not* die, and *to live:* it helps us work out how to live with conflict and desire.

But Julian, I'm a Little Bit Older Than You

Emily Pope

I've never told anyone this before but,
I used to masturbate to
But Julian, I'm a little bit older than you
by Courtney Love, three times a night in the hope that one of my housemates would walk in on me so that they would know that I was a woman with sexual agency and not just - single - and dull.
For context, here are a few lines from the song:
I'm overrated, desecrated
Still somehow illuminated
I know I've got a screw loose
Just meet me in the bedroom

Last night, in the bedroom, I had a dream. In the dream I felt like I was going to be sick. Instead of being sick I had to pull a lot of long silver fish out of my mouth and then put them in the stream by the side of the road, as I was on a road trip. My friend told me that fish lived in everyone's stomachs and that I should relax about it, and I accepted this fact.

The next section of the dream was that I was driving to a swimming pool and I had to swim whilst thinking about the scene from *Dallas Buyers Club* where Jared Leto's character Rayon coughs up loads of blood before dying of AIDS, and once I had done the laps required to contemplate this I was allowed to go through to the next stage, which was watching live performance art in a sports stadium.

In the sports stadium there was a woman singing and yelling on a trapeze doing a loud and typical takedown of all socioeconomic structures, whilst wearing a cheerleading outfit. The whole thing was getting a bit *Bring It On,* when she surprised everyone by doing the splits in mid air and staying in the splits. There was a glass sculpture on the ground which looked like a line of jagged blades of grass in exactly the right place. She stayed in the splits and landed directly on the broken glass sculpture from a great height, and the performance finished and I could hear sirens in the distance.

Then I woke up.

From this I can conclude that I have been thinking about the self sacrificial (messianic) trends I have observed in recent performance art, and I think that I can conclude from my dream that these don't turn me on in the same way that Courtney Love does.

Anyway - I've never told anyone *this* before either but, sometimes I really think that Fred West had the right idea, the Moors murderers had the right idea - have you seen Maxine Peake in *See No Evil*, she really is an excellent actress - and I do believe *in some respects,* not all, *obviously*, that murder is an art form and - I - I - need to check you aren't recording me. I don't air these thoughts regularly and I don't like to talk about my dreams very much either - I am worried if I talk about them, then they immediately belong to someone else.

I've never told anyone this before but, once I pretended someone had stolen my bag because I had completely run out of money, and I knew that meant someone would have to sub me twenty quid until I got a new card, and this was less embarrassing than just admitting I had run out of money.

I've never told you this before but all of the manipulative moves that you pull, and tiny lies you have told, which you think are incredibly subtle, well, I can see you doing them and know how your voice changes when you tell them, and it exhausts me so I just let you carry on whilst I think about other things - like emigrating.

I've never told anyone this before but, my step-dad quite often kisses me on the lips and he only does it when my Mum isn't in the room. I'm twenty-five and this has been going on for ten years and I just thought you looked.. er.. non-judgemental and I just wondered...do you think I should say anything?

I've never told anyone this before but, he has been sleeping with prostitutes for twenty years, My mum left him, and I feel guilty because I met up with him last week because, pathetically or not, I feel sorry for him and it is *doing my head in* because I keep thinking if I was a genuinely loyal person I would want nothing to do with him.

I've never told anyone this before but, I had the realisation the other day when someone was saying 'oh god if I took tramadol everyday I would really start to lose it', you know... he said that before dinner and you looked at me and winked... well it isn't really that funny because I've started to lose it for *exactly that reason*, and that is the reason I cried whilst we were watching *The Producers*, it had absolutely nothing to do with me finding *The Producers* incredibly funny.

I've never told anyone this before but, I have all these whatsapp messages in files and I need to print them out because I need to take them to the Embassy to prove we actually regularly talk so that we can get married over here. I also need to delete some of the messages from the whatsapp file because they are too rude for the Embassy to read, I would be *really* embarrassed if they read them!

I've never told anyone this before but, you know on the overground when I yelled YOU MAKE ME FEEL SICK at a man because he touched me inappropriately, and the carriage cheered and I came home with prosecco, well, I think he just brushed against me accidentally because it was so crowded but I really fancied a shout and it's always good to make that particular point, isn't it? People who never speak up will benefit from the example and I bet the man didn't even think about it afterwards.

I've never told anyone this before but, I keep thinking that the illuminati are real and I used to love Angelina Jolie and now everytime I look at her I see a serpent - will you stop laughing.

I've never told anyone this before but I got given a necklace as a gift and it made my neck go green so I took it to the shop and complained and they said - look, sorry, but the reason your neck is green is because you are sweating alcohol, and that is - er - eroding some of the metal. Sorry. You cannot have a refund.

I've never told anyone this before but, my gran was room temperature when she died and I felt so weird for noticing when really I should have been too upset to notice.

I've never told anyone this before but, once we arranged to have someone's hand chopped off and now he has a hook for a hand, and we are still friends and I've done a lot of things I could be put inside for, which I am sure you've worked out.

I've never told anyone this before but I've done SIXTY TWO job applications this year and I've been hoping that this bus I am on (from London to a regional gallery) crashes and all these middle class pen pushers just die, and it gets in the *Daily Mail.*

I've never told anyone this before but I've written it down, multiple times -

I pay 600 pounds a month in rent if I am lucky, I am educated, I am complicit, I live like I am on the dole in the 80's with the added horror of the internet and there are too many manifestos lapping up on my screen for me to write a new one and for it to be profound, so I suggest - *just lying down* on the floor for a year and withdrawing all labour, all cultural capital and all making until the creative industries with all of their (thinly veiled by their poster children) conservatism, sexism, racism, homophobia, transphobia and classism grind to a satisfying halt and then we can rebuild something different, chaotic and fierce which comes from love. I mean it. What about time to think? What about rejection of precarity? What about Just Not Working? No more events no more fundraisers no more performances no more pretending to be more traumatised than you are to capitalise on an identity, whilst skillfully ignoring the marginalisation you are *actually* facing due to your economic reality, patriarchal heteronormativity enforced by capitalism, and the fact that you are a symptom of hyperreality. What about no longer being complicit in a cycle of labour that will at some point make you just as hideous as your boss?

I've never told anyone this before but I have become desensitised to just how hideous *I* am, I've realised when it is too late and the guilt has started to eat me. I wonder what happens to the body if you lie on the floor for a whole year in your own piss and shit... would you start to disintegrate due to the moisture from the piss and shit like when your fingertips go like prunes in the bath? Would people feed you and water you - probably not as people do not do that for the homeless very often - do you think that the headline would be: *2018, the year everyone needed to be sectioned including the psychiatrists and psychoanalysts, because everyone just decided to lie down on the floor and never get up again*?

I Swallow Your Pride

Charan Singh

'I swallow' he said.
'Swallow what?'

'Your pride!'
'Ouch! No, I thought we are doing vanilla.'

'It is, but with a little twist. And it's me who is taking. I am not asking for anything in return.'
'Alright, if that makes you happy.' He smirked.

Such a jerk, as if he's doing a favour for me. Sanjay is right about these pretentious 'total-tops'.
Argh... he bends on his knees.
Gasp, hmm... such a smelly man. I so wanted to grow a mushroom such as this; in my mouth for so long!

His favourite song had stopped in the middle and then there was the news update on the radio, a sign of the turning of an hour. That made him realise – 'Oh, it's 7 o'clock, *paani chala jayega* (the water will go off). I must get ready for work'. He gets up, takes a peaceful dump, followed by a shower, has breakfast and then leaves for work with plenty of time in hand on this glorious morning.

Every morning, he takes the bus number 611 at 8:13am. Which goes via Chand Cinema, Sarai Kale Khan, Nehru Place, Lajpat Nagar, Arsham, and terminates at Daula Kuan. On a smooth-traffic day, it takes about an hour and twenty minutes from Mayur Vihar to reach to Safdarjung, where he works. He normally likes to sit on a window seat but today he only got an aisle. After a while the bus got busy and by this time people started pushing to get in, some are hanging at the door, holding the ledge. This is when he realises that a solid object is pressing against his shoulder. He couldn't look at it but he is thinking about what that thing might be? And then...

Dear Diary,
Today my bus was really packed; one could not lift one's hand to hold the bar, if one hadn't already. Not sure if it was my luck or not, but I think I nearly touched his crotch in the bus.

Amit makes eye contact with him, and he left the rest for their eyes to negotiate.

'Looks like you're getting excited.'
'Who, me?'
'Ah ha...'
He cleared his throat and replied awkwardly, 'Um...Yeah that happens sometimes. My excitement doesn't wait for an invitation. It gets aroused, just like that'.
'No worries, darling, I'll help you, if you will let me. Would you like to share my seat?'

Amit crosses his legs and nods his head as a gesture offering half of the seat to sit with him. And so, he sits on the edge. Amit put one hand across his shoulder and holds him tight so that he doesn't fall and other hand he puts on his thighs. Then he lures him into a conversation.
'Oh, nice pants, where did you get this fabric? It feels so good and comfortable!' And both smile.

Every time the bus crosses over a bump, Amit's hand reaches out further, and beyond. Soon Amit's hand started exploring the landscapes of the other's manhood. And on the next bump -
'Goddamn it - they never fix Delhi's road, do they?' He rants, while rolling his eyes.

Oops, I have been trying to get his attention for weeks. Never mind the clumsiness, at least, he noticed and I got more than what I expected. Life is good.
I can give you a kiss today.
Mwah!

Dear Diary,
Today I walked to Sanjay's house. I like him but he has very weird ideas about 'hand-practice'. I thought everyone does it, in fact it is the best *'time-pass'* for a summer's day. In winter, everything shrinks and nothing blossoms. Anyway, he said that I should be careful about getting my sperm on my hands and not to use only one hand too much, otherwise it will bend towards the other. How on earth that could happen? I have no idea. He was showing me a booklet which says that each drop of sperm is made up of forty drops of blood, so

technically we are shedding a lot of blood into the drain; each time. He was also telling me that we can become deaf, impotent or blind. We should protect ourselves and our country from getting weak. Personally, I don't think it'll make us deaf or anything. Otherwise, Ramesh uncle would have been all those things by now. I see him very often on the roof, pleasuring himself.
Bye-bye now,
Amit.

One day, Amit decided to follow him. Amit got off the bus after him. He went into a park, but Amit was a bit apprehensive to follow him inside, instead he stood outside the park. But then few minutes later...

'Hawa Main Udta Jaye Mera Laal Dupatta Malmal Ka, Ho Jee... Ho Jee...' (Be My Red Muslin Scarf that Flies in the Air, Oh Listen...) A young, pretty boy walked past Amit, singing this famous song from a 1950s Bollywood movie. His voice was like melting sugar in his ear.

Amit's fascination to hear a little more of that pretty boy, made him follow the boy inside the park, where there were a lot of men roaming around, all behaving strangely. A lot of these men were just staring at each other, and a few were whispering. Some were disappearing and reappearing from the bushes as if they were under the spell of some supernatural power, just like in science fiction movies. It was very peculiar to see this. Then one man smirked at him and slurred 'First time, huh'. He felt alive again.

Dear Diary,
Today I am sitting alone in the park. I feel sad. It is bit like *Kishor ke dard bhare nagme* (heart-wrenching songs by Kishor Kumar) echoing in my head but without the melodrama of (Indian) cinema. A week ago, I met a foreigner in the park who liked me - I liked him. We had fun at his hotel, for the first time on a bed. It was pure fun without talking much. I mean we spoke through our bodies and senses, however, we couldn't use our spoken languages. But imagine a foreigner who doesn't speak English, although I don't either but at least I could've said, '*hi-hello*'. All he says is '*merci ma chérie*' every time I help (blow) him and I just 'giggle' when he helps me. It is very bad that, we don't speak the same language and in this situation of mine, (the 16th century poet) Amir Khusro comes to mind -

> The language of my beloved is Turkish, and Turkish I do not know!
> Would it not be wonderful if his tongue were in my mouth!!

Ab bus (that's it now).

His favourite song had stopped in the middle and then there was the news update on the radio - a sign of the turning of an hour. That made him realise – 'Oh, it's 7 o'clock, *paani chala jayega* (the water will go off). I must get ready for work'. So, he gets up, takes a peaceful dump, followed by a shower, has breakfast and leaves for work with plenty of time in hand. This was his notion of an ideal morning to start the day. But of course, his mornings never turn out the way he imagines them to be. Instead, he often runs out of water which results in him taking a bucket bath, due to the delay there is not much time for breakfast and you will see him running behind the buses, trying to catch them. He catches them nonetheless and that is where the story begins...

In his dream; he keeps a diary, in which, occasionally he writes - once upon a time there was a young man, named *Amit*.

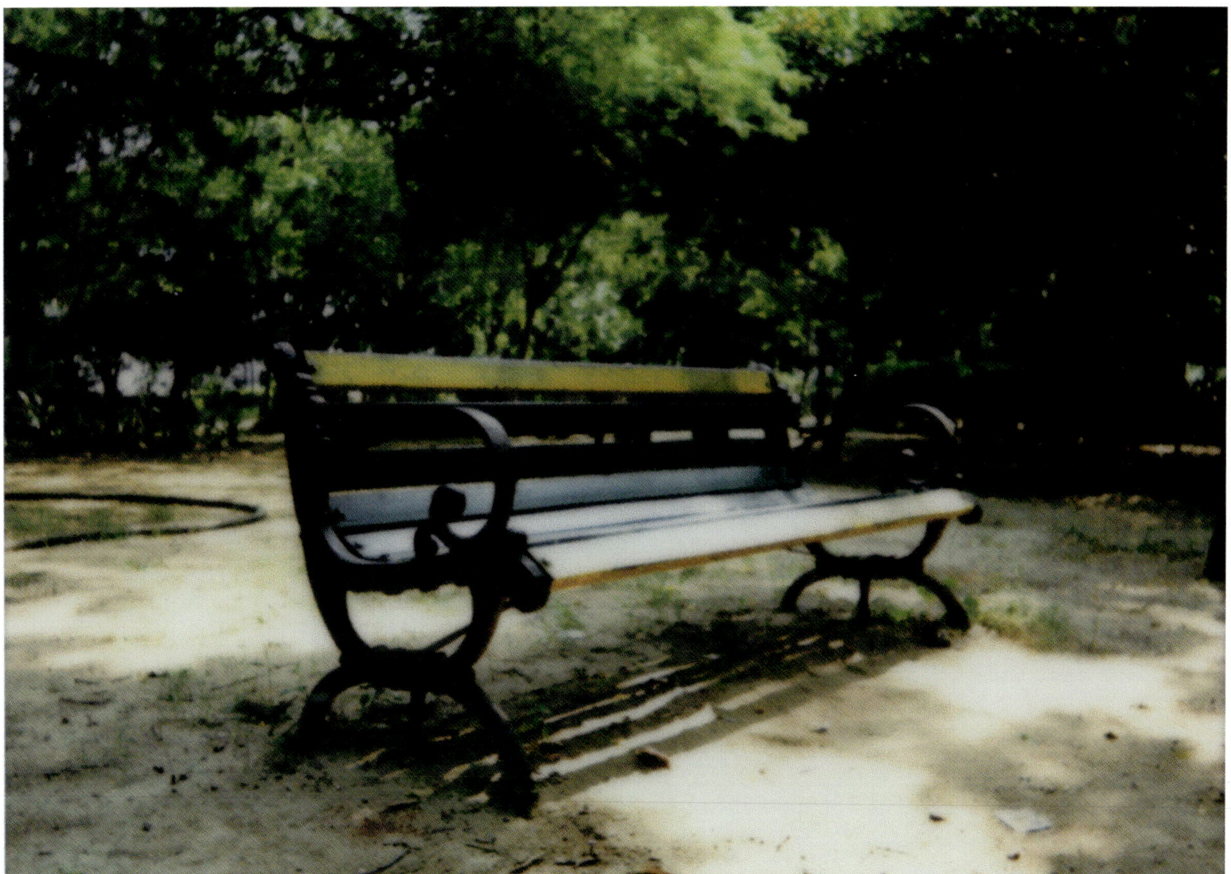

Not all office cleaners are middle aged Mrs Mops. Some firms hire quite young and beautiful girls to work early evening cleaning offices out. Linda is such a girl…

THE OFFICE CLEANER

It was a one off job. The office was really a bed sitter rented by a writer. He was going away for the day and rang up my firm asking them to send someone to clean his place up. They sent me! The place was a terrible mess when I started, but after an hour I had it as smart as a new pin. As I said, it was more of a bed sitter than an office. A typewriter was on a desk, but there was also a bed. It looked as though the writer also lived in his office. When everything was cleaned up I sat on the edge of the bed, wondering what Mr James wrote about. I am an extremely nosy person, so I opened a desk drawer and took out some manuscript. My eyes boggled as I read the first few pages. It was all about sex, and horny stuff it was to. I felt my juices begin to bubble as I read and read, the descriptions were so vivid, I could almost feel the girl's emotions as the handsome man screwed her. Then I found some photographs, pin-ups I believe they are called. The girls were quite pretty, but not as good looking as me, nor were their figures as good. I would make a good model! What with the pictures and the reading, I was feeling very sexy. I looked at my watch, it was only seven thirty, I hadn't any more work to do, I might as well enjoy myself!

I undressed as slowly as I could, swaying my body so that my breasts bounced up and down, as if tormenting a man. When I was naked I sat on the bed, my legs wide apart, and examined my dark haired pussy. I have a nice pussy, at least that is what my boy friends tell me. I get wet very quickly, in fact a kiss is enough to make me dribble, so you can imagine the state of it after reading all that sex stuff. I pulled the labia lips apart and gently rubbed over my clit. Yes, I thought, I will make a good model. I was going along very nicely, my fingers moving swiftly in and out of my hole, when I heard a noise outside. I sat up quickly, wiping my sticky fingers on the sheet, and reached for my clothes. I was too late, the door opened and in walked a man. He stared at me in disbelief, blinked a couple of times, then spoke.

"And who are you?" he asked.

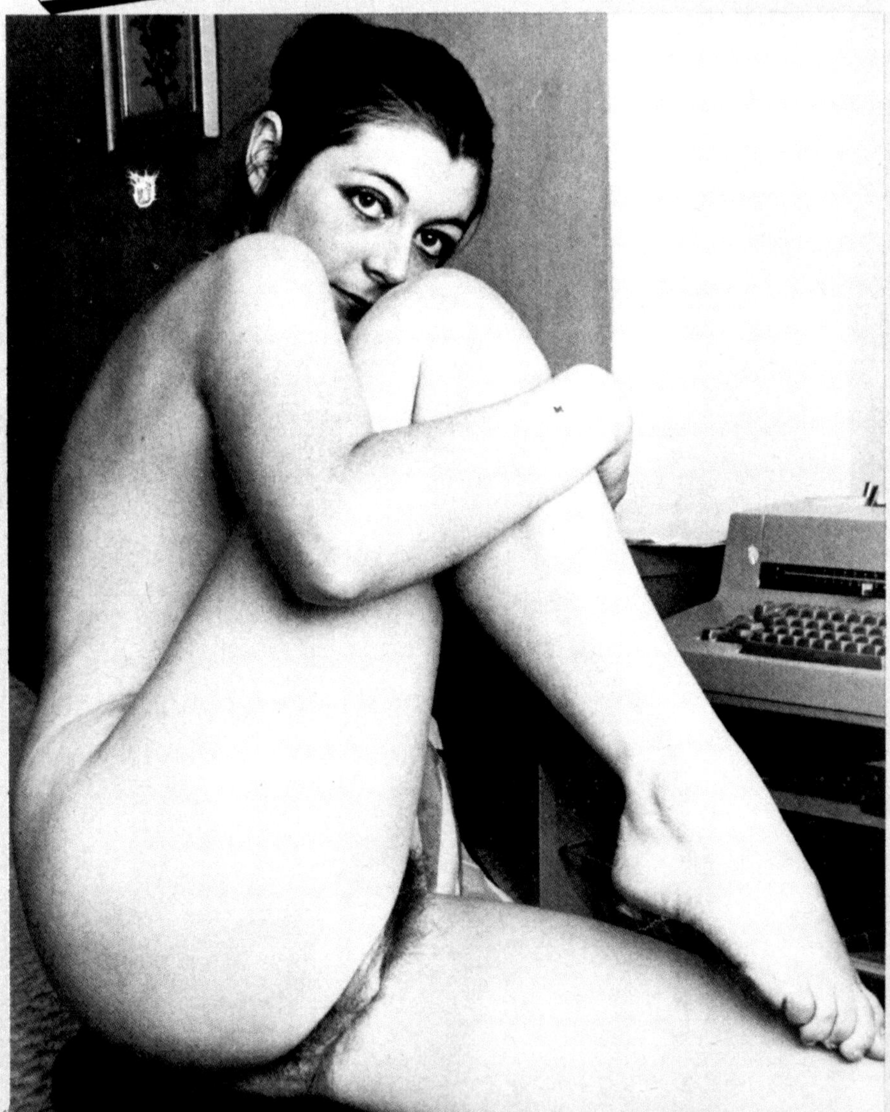

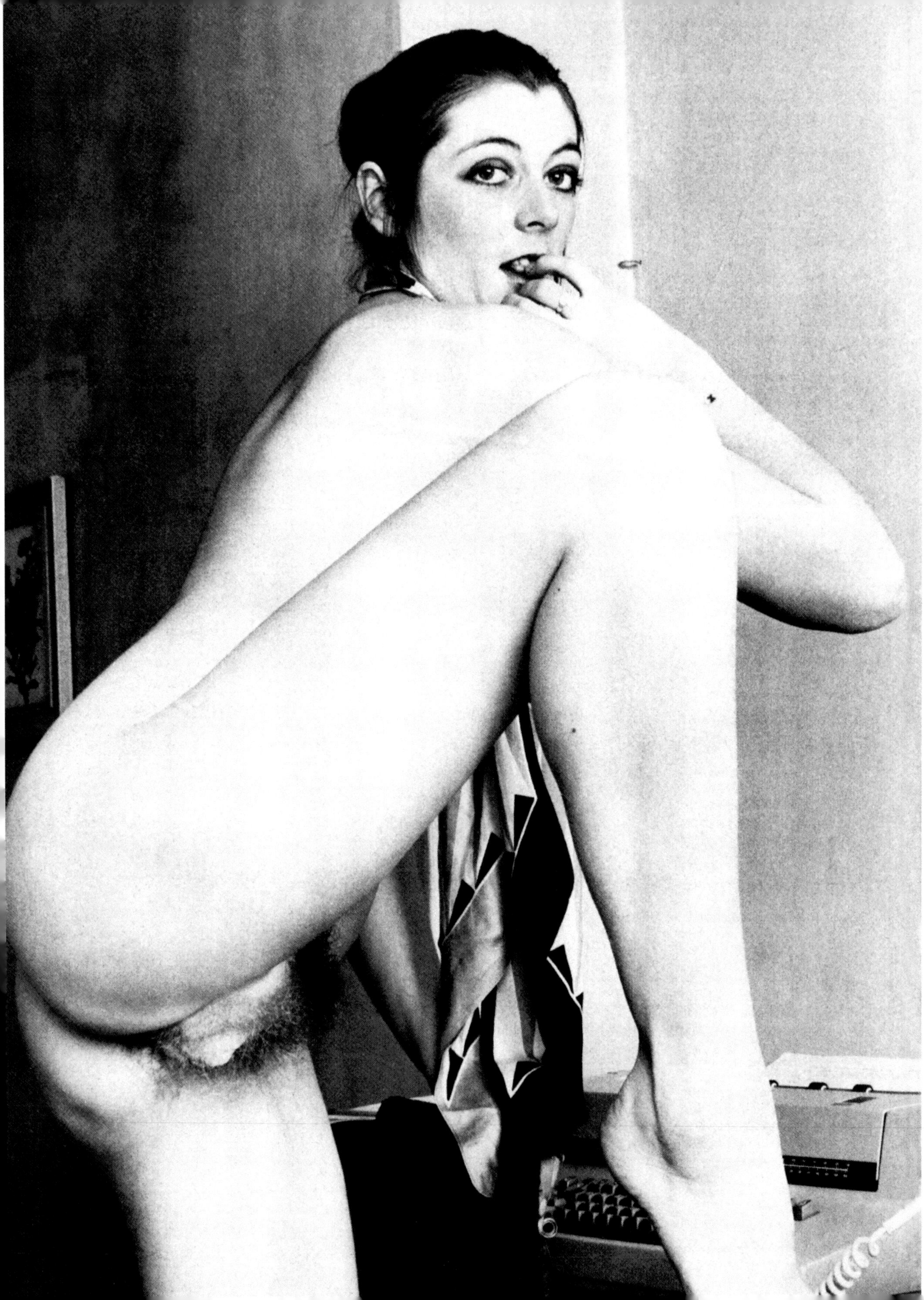

I gulped, pulling a sheet over my nakedness. "I... I am the office cleaner, sent round to tidy your office."

He glanced at the photographs, strewn over the bed, then at the manuscripts on the floor.

"If I had known they sent naked office cleaners out, I would have sent for you before!"

"Oh, it was just that... well, I saw some of these pictures, and decided to have some fun with myself."

He came across to the bed and pulled the sheet away from me, I put my hands over my breasts trying to cover them up, but I couldn't hide my pussy at the same time.

"You certainly have a lovely body," he murmured, "nicely shaped breasts, good thighs and from what bit I can see, a rounded bottom! I'd like to take your photograph, if you have no objections.

"You mean in the nude, like those girls are?"

He nodded, the cheeky devil touching my bare breast.

"With my legs open, showing my pussy?"

He nodded again, this time openly caressing my left tit. I looked straight at his fly, there was a promising bulge there. I'm a sucker if a guy gets a hard on in front of me, and I meant that in every sense of the word.

"Very well," I murmured, conscious that my tit was getting hard under his hand. "Get your camera Mr. James."

"Call me Barry," he said, reluctantly removing his hand from my left mammary. "Lay on that bed as though a man is going to give you some hard cock."

He certainly got straight to the point, I was left in no doubt the kind of pose he wanted. I sprawled on the bed, knees bent and apart, my fanny wide open and tried to imagine a hard dick about to ram up. My imagination was so good that as Barry got his camera and flash ready I tickled my tits, making the nipples harden. He turned round, liked what he saw, and took a couple of photographs.

I posed all over the place, on his desk, by the typewriter. I was so close to it once that the space bar tickled my pussy! He seemed fascinated by my bottom, making me stick it out so that he could get some good pictures of it. Mind you, most men like my bottom, saying that it holds the mysteries of the Universe. I don't know what they mean by that. He must have taken a hundred pictures of me, most with my legs open, and me playing with my tits. I was getting very randy with all this nakedness, and when he wasn't looking, I kept frigging at my slit.

When he had put his camera away I sat on the bed, still naked of course. I wanted to be screwed, and Barry was a presentable young man, he'd had a hard on once, he could get a hard on again!

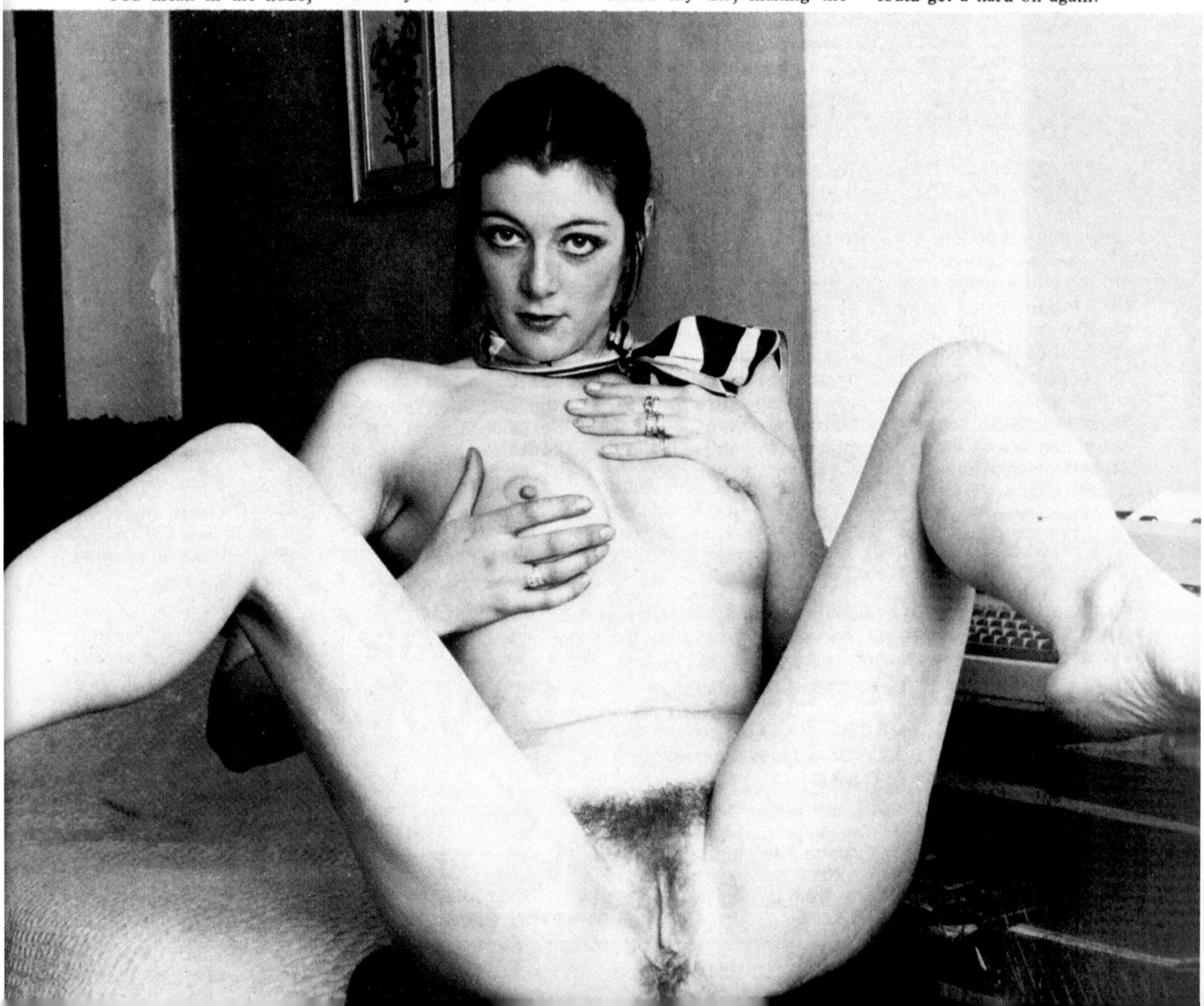

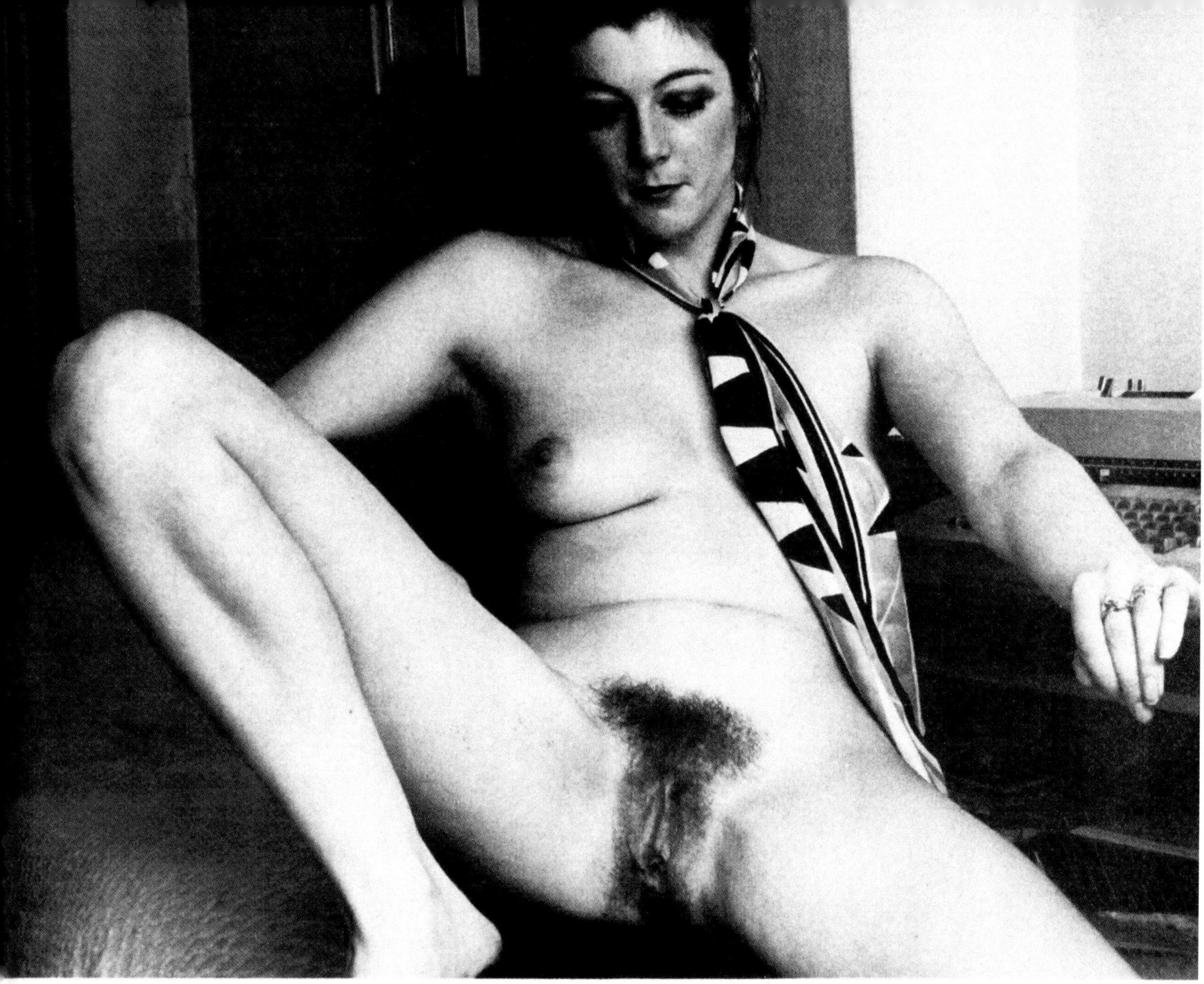

He sat by my side. "I'll pay you twenty pounds for posing for me," he smiled. "Did you enjoy it?"

I said that I did, and snuggled close to him, my tit resting on his shoulder as he lay back on the bed. He smiled up at me and unzipped his fly. His half hard cock nestled in his groin so I lifted it out carefully with a hooked finger, and held it in the palm of my hand. I didn't have to do any rubbing, it stiffened without any help. He put his hands behind his head, still grinning at me as I played around with the knob end. I squeezed it a few times until drops of clear moisture appeared at the eye. I squeezed, opening the eye up, then I put the point of my tongue against it. He grunted with pleasure, so I did it again, slowly wanking him at the same time. I kept it up for about five minutes until I was bored. I'd suck him off later, if he wished, but at that moment I wanted to be caressed first, then well screwed. I unbuckled his belt and pulled his trousers down. It took me five minutes to get his shirt away, he kept pulling me over him, kissing my tits and trying to get his cock up my pussy. When he was naked I half lay across him, my thighs apart so that I could rub my juicy hole on his leg. I caressed his tits with mine, and run my hand into his groin, making the nerves jump and his cock rear harder. He was very pleased with the way I was making love with him, and he told me so. His prick was doing a lot of weeping, so I slowed my hand movements down, I didn't want him coming all over the place.

Suddenly he asked me if I fancied a bit across the desk, just a few strokes to get us in the mood. I was already in the mood, but I fancied a few strokes. I placed my hands flat on the desk and stuck my bum out. He came behind me, stroking his wet cock over my bottom, and fondling it at the same time. I told him I wasn't having any bottom screwing, it hurts. He had no intention of doing that, he said he preferred the proper place every time. He placed his cock between my open legs and pushed it up and down the slit, not going inside, but doing enough to make me suddenly orgasm. He held me close to him, his cock wedged in my crevice, his hands cupping my tits. When I had calmed down, he started to stroke along me again, his ridge rasping

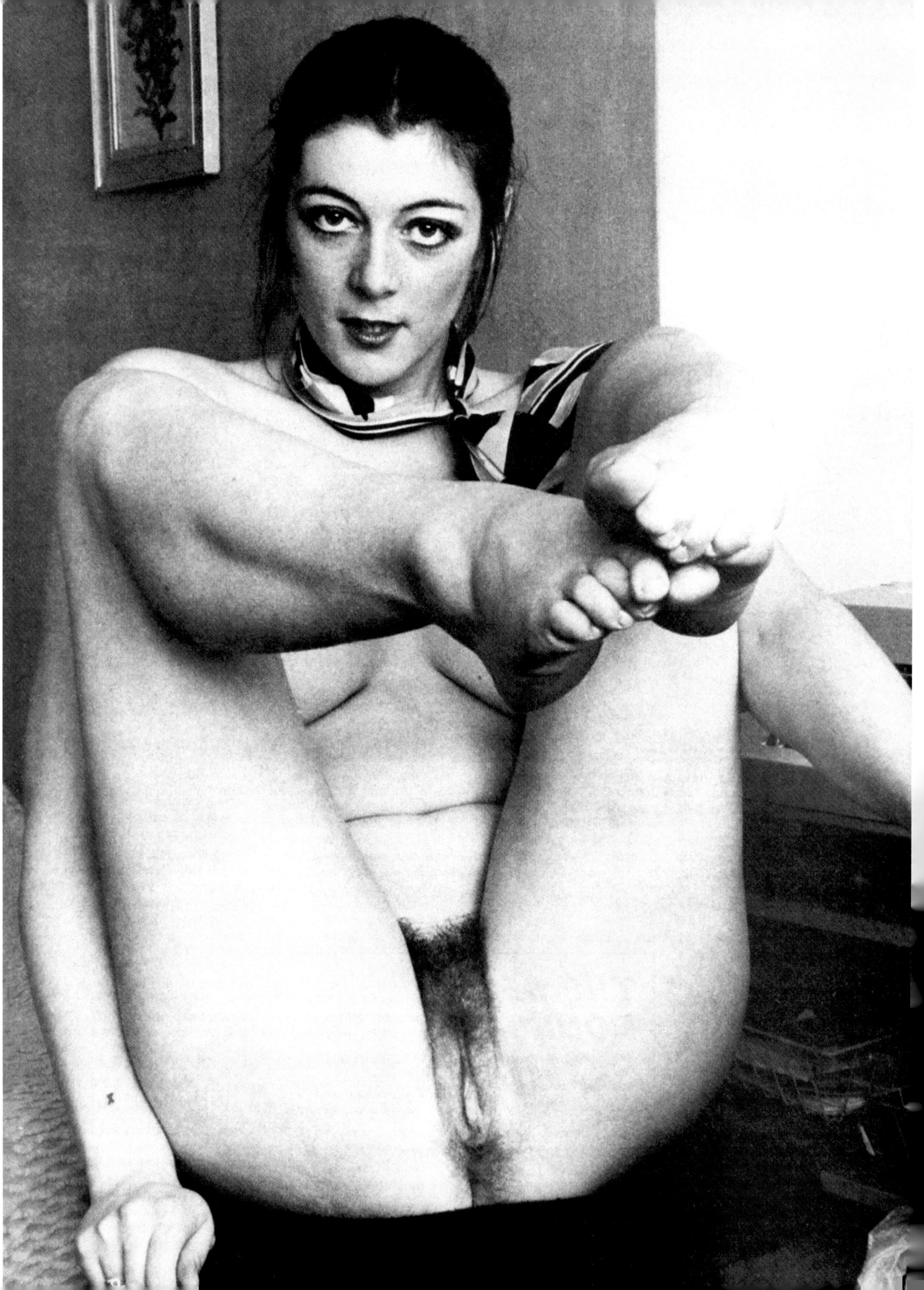

against my tender clit. I don't know about other girls, but when I have climaxed, my clit is sore, and the constant friction against it was rather painful, so I asked him if he would mind stopping for a while.

"But I haven't shot off sweetheart, don't you think you are being a bit unfair?"

I assured him that I was being unfair, and if he would lie on the bed I'd look after his cock in other ways.

It took me all my time to stop from laughing as he walked across to the bed, his cock waving about in front of him. I think men look funny when they are naked, thin spindly legs, a funny bottom, and their most precious possession sticking out from their belly. He lay down on the bed, slowly wanking himself. I waited a few moments, he could bring himself off like that. But he realised what he was doing and beckoned me to join him.

I squatted on my haunches and blew warm air over his throbbing erection. The underside of his tool was a deep purple, he was in a right old state, dying to shoot off and get some relief. Tenderly I took his weapon in my hand, playing with it, squeezing it, then sucking it. I have tasted many things in my life, but nothing can compare with the taste of a guy's cock when it has been shafting a girl's passage. It isn't distasteful, in fact it is rather nice, sort of salty. I edged my teeth just below the ridge, and flapped my tongue on the helmet. I must have bitten rather hard because his hips jumped up, almost throwing me away! So I took him into my throat, fondling his ball bag at the same time. He liked that, and began a gentle flow, up and down, with his hips. I thought I would tease him a bit, so I plopped him from my lips and kissed his inner thighs, working my way down his leg until I reached his feet. I took his big toe and rubbed it, much in the same way as I would have rubbed his prick. He stared down at me in amazement, wondering what the hell I was doing. When I got his toe between my legs, wedging it in my wet hole, he caught on, and wriggled it around. His tool was still verging on the point of coming, so I moved up, his toe still in my hole, and

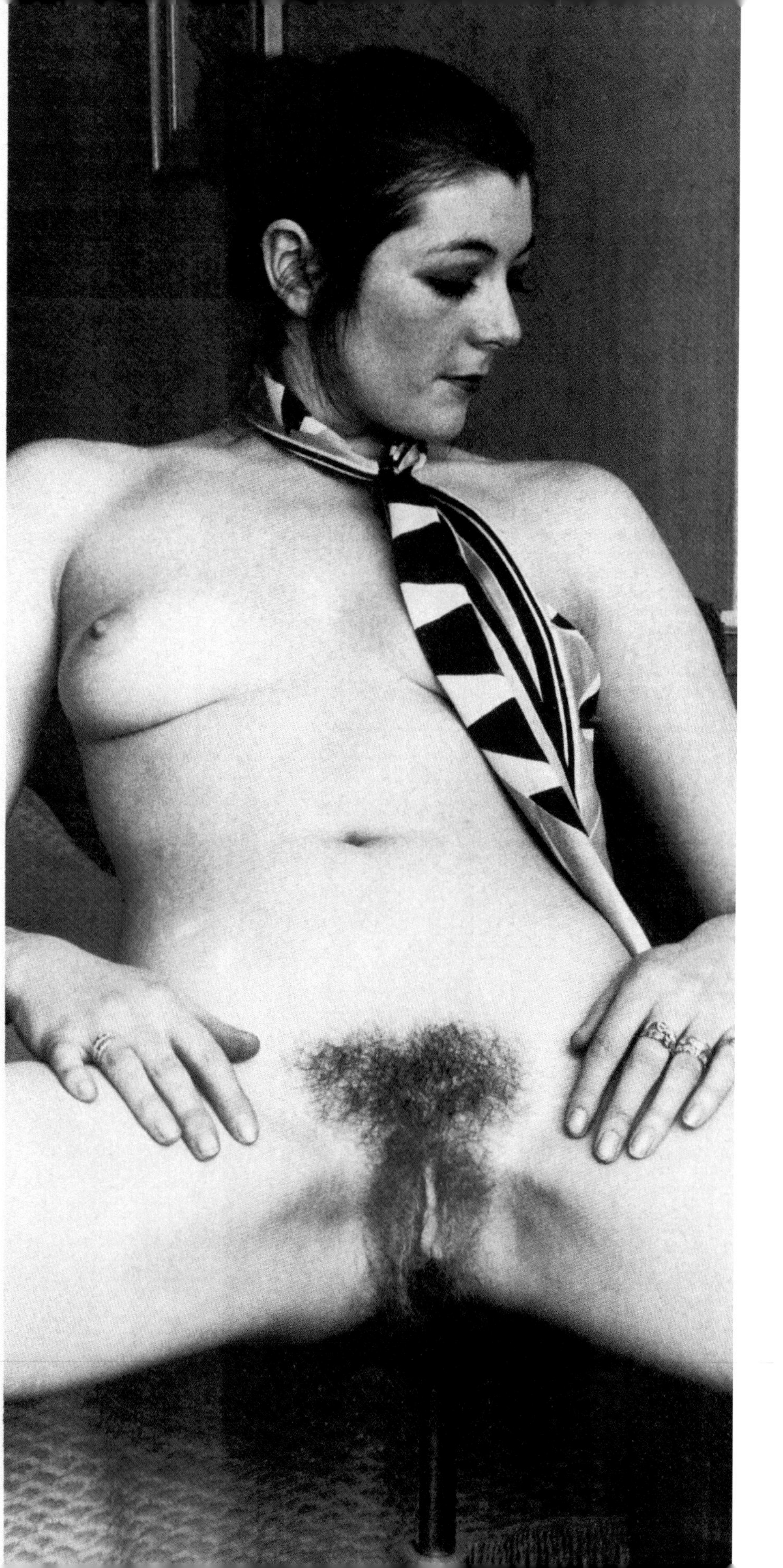

kissed and sucked it for him. Suddenly his hips jerked, and all his come was shooting into my mouth, gallons of the stuff, coming and coming until with a long sigh he relaxed and took his toe out.

"There," I murmured, "I told you I would look after your cock!"

I spent the next half hour wandering around his office, sprawling on his desk, playing with my pussy, and reading his dirty stories at the same time. He was certainly a horny guy, the things he could think about made the mind boggle. I wondered if he was married, and how his wife coped with his sexuality.

"Linda," he said, flicking his cock at me, trying to tempt me to suck him again. "If I did all the things I wrote about, I would have had an early death, fucked out of my mind and body! It is rare that I get the chance to practice what I preach, so come back here on the bed, I want to try something out!"

I joined him a bit warily, I once had a right old time with a kinky bloke, all he wanted to do was feed peanuts into my slit and watch me thrust them out! I also once read about a pop star who had put a Mars bar in his girl friend's hole, and then ate it. Now that would have been rather nice, his mouth licking away at the chocolate!

"What do you want to try?" I asked.

"I want to see if I can make you come just by playing with your tits!" he grinned. "A guy was telling me the other day that he could make a girl shoot for the moon just by sucking and playing with her tits. I don't think it is possible, a girl must require cunt stimulation as well."

The man was getting worse, talking like that, yet, the thought of him playing around with my tits for a long time appealed to me. You see I love having my breasts played with, not like Doris, one of the cleaners where I work. She can't stand being touched on her tits, makes her shudder and go right off.

"Okay," I said, "here I come, do your best."

I prostrated myself by his side, breasts pushed well up, waiting for attention. First of all he breathed on me, then wiggled his fingers over the nipple.

"Look Barry," I murmured, taking hold of his hand and placing it on my ripe mound. "You'll never make me come like that. Brush up and over my breasts, then when your hand is high, suck the nipple, not for long, then bring your hand back down. No!, don't squeeze it like an orange, be gentle. I'll tell you when to start the rough stuff."

I lay half on my side, facing him, and he used both his hands on my tits, stroking up, then lingering while he kissed each nipple in turn. To give myself more excitement I took his hard cock in my hand and slowly wanked him. My tits got harder, the nipples beginning to ache under his caress. Christ, but I wanted to be screwed, but I held back, and kept my thighs together, I was assisting in an important experiment. If he was successful in making me orgasm, then he could write an article about it, and thousands of girls all over the world would be able to come even when they couldn't fuck!

I could feel the skin tightening on my breasts as he played with them, the nipple turning blood red as he

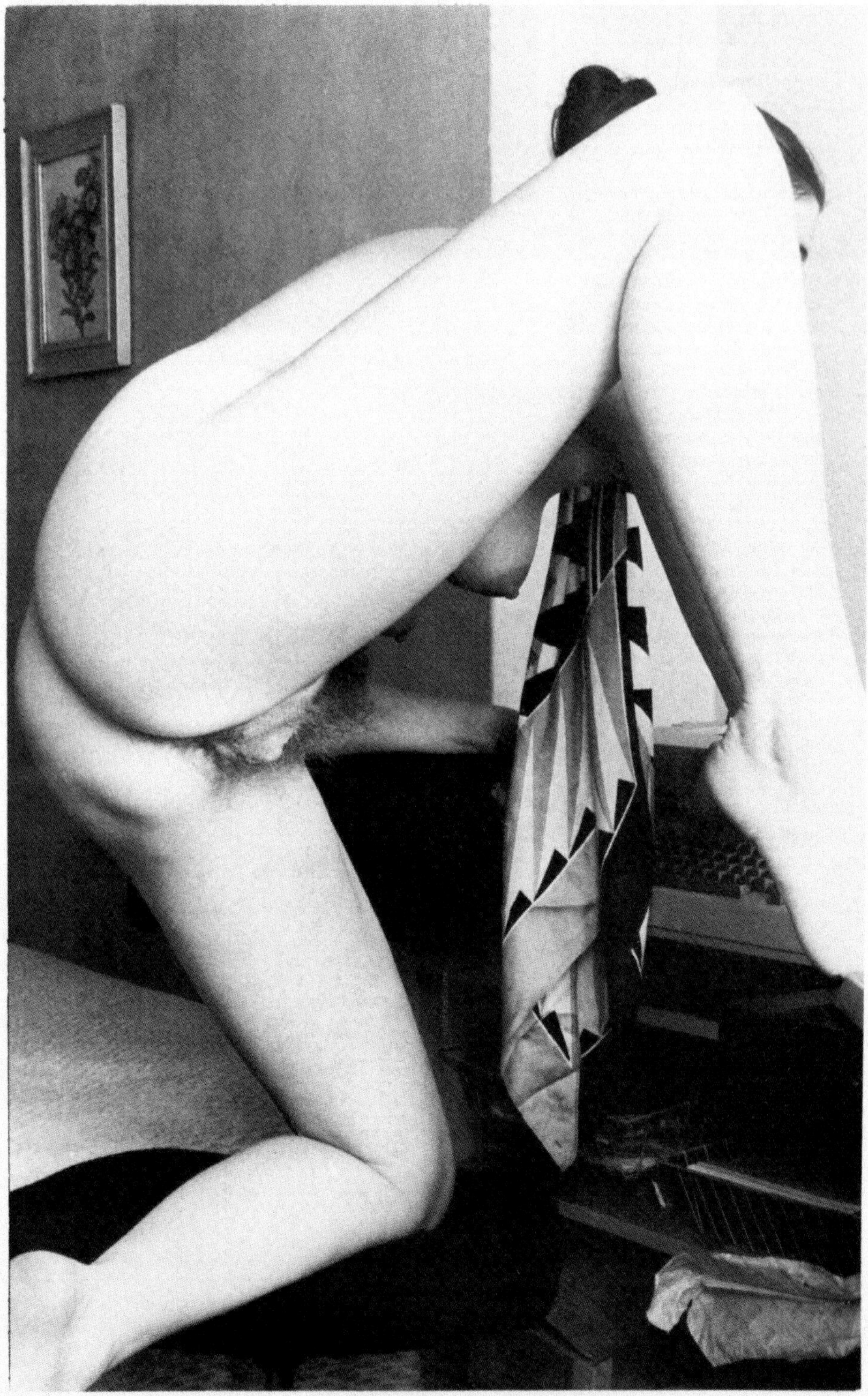

rasped his tongue on it. His cock was weeping all over my thigh, and he kept jerking his hips against me. I debated whether or not to toss him off and let him spunk, but if I did that, all his interest would go, he would only be play acting as he fondled my boobs. I am susceptible to atmosphere, I can't get turned on if my man has lost interest in what he is doing.

Then the strangest thing happened. What he was doing to my tits transmitted down my nervous system to my hole, delicious churnings started inside me, I could feel my clit stiffening, and I had to keep a tight hold on his cock to keep my hand away from my pussy. So I squeezed my thighs together, then relaxed them, that helped I can tell you. Barry was panting like a dog after a run in the hot sun, his hips moving rapidly so that my hand slipped up and down his hard prick. I closed my eyes, imagining him fucking me, his large red cock creeping towards my hole. It had the desired effect, my fanny trembled.

"I'm going to come," I grunted. "God, I'm going to come!"

And I did, but the horrible part was, there was nothing inside me when I did, I ached to feel a hard dick thrusting in, or even a couple of fingers, but there was nothing, just the shivers inside my vagina as I orgasmed.

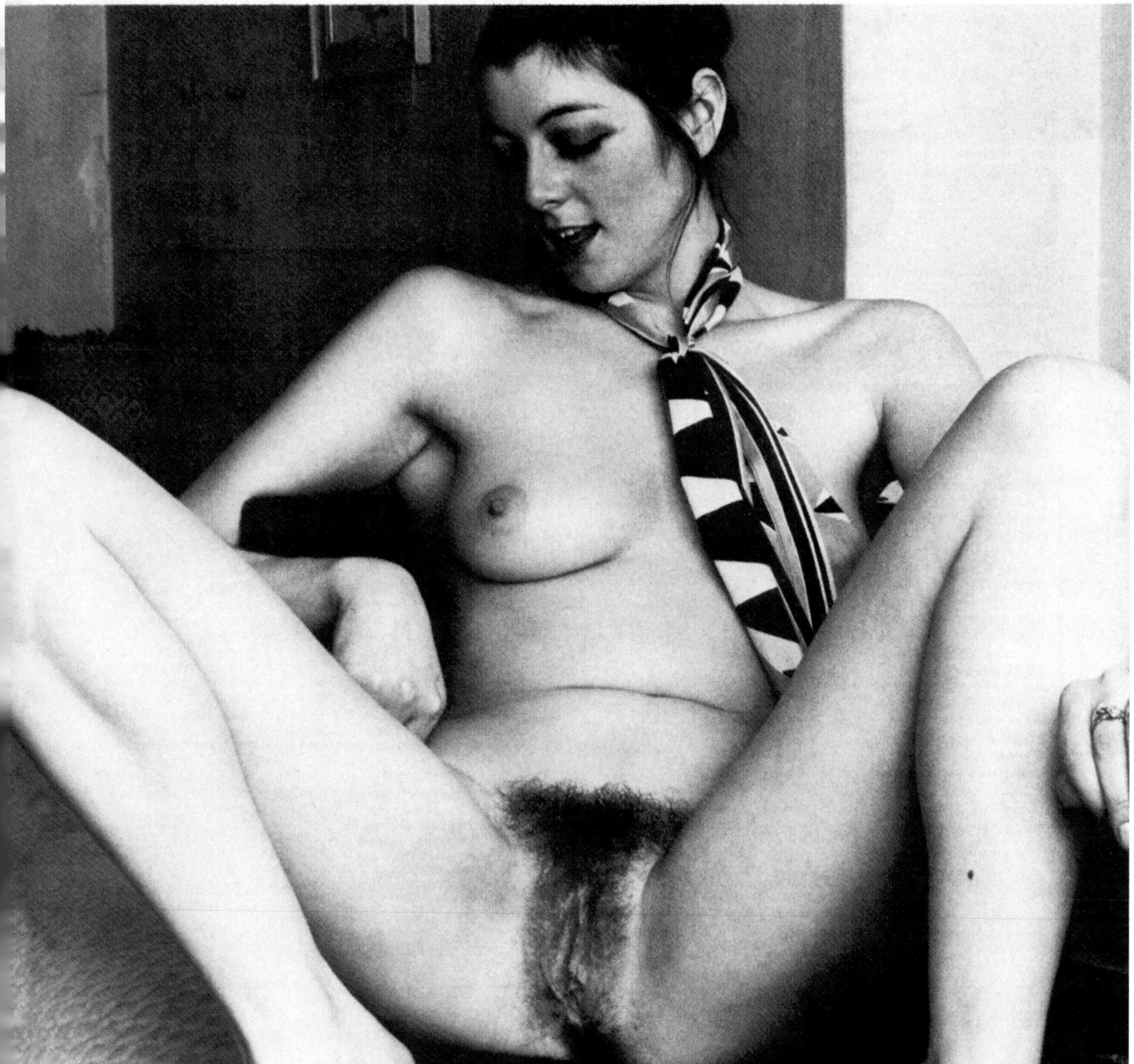

Barry had a look of triumph on his face as he gazed down at me. "It works," he shouted, "for Christ's sake, it works! Open your legs Linda, my old man is ready for bursting."

I opened up and he came over me, sliding deeply in. Ah, but it felt good, even though I had only just orgasmed. He screwed me for about thirty seconds before he groaned, pushed in deep as his tool swelled up, and he shot off.

The pair of us were shattered after that, his cock was like a sausage ready for the frying pan, and I felt to be drained. My nipples and breasts were sore, they'd had more attention during the last half hour than they'd had during the last twelve months! I touched them carefully, then took my hand away, they really hurt me. I decided that all that tit massaging was not for me, even though I did come. You can't beat a proper screwing, plenty of foreplay, but a big prick riding home in the end.

Barry had fallen asleep, so I surmised that he was done for the night. He'd screwed, he'd been chewed off, he'd played with my breasts for a long time. What more could any man ask of me. I climbed from the bed and started to pull on my black panties. He opened his eyes.

"You're not going yet," he said, "there is the night before us."

"I couldn't stand any more breast massage sweetheart," I said softly.

"Relax Linda, come back here, open your legs and let me kiss between them. I promise you I won't touch your breasts, ever again. I want to kiss you until you come, then take your photograph."

The man was positively obscene, was scared of nothing. However, I got back on the bed, leaving my panties on the floor, and once again stretched out, waiting for his lustful attentions.

"This is going to be a two way job," he said, frankly. "You come over me, legs apart so that I can look up into the box. As I eat you, you eat me, and we'll see if we can make it together."

I had nothing to lose, so I straddled his face, lowering myself down until I could feel his mouth on my secret cave. For the first few minutes I didn't feel much emotion, just the gentle licking of his tongue, but when I took his half hard cock and placed it in my mouth the urge came back my loins shuddered as his tongue delved deeper. I rocked my hips over his face as he hungrily mouthed my pussy, and I sucked his now hard cock. This was turning into quite a night. I had come to clean an office, not indulge in a sex jamboree! He came very swiftly, and I pulled him out, pressing his cock against my sore tits, the balm flooding out helping to soothe them I rammed my fanny down hard on his mouth, almost screaming when I came.

I got home at ten o'clock, well screwed and happy, even though I was walking stiff-legged. My husband asked me why I was so late.

"You should have seen this office darling," I said. "It was filthy, it took me ages to clean the place up."

"You should ask for more money," he grumbled. "Working until this time. I fancied a jump. You ought to see this book I've been reading."

I took the book from his hand.

"Jump For Joy," I read out, "by Barry James."

"He must have done some screwing around," said my husband, fondling my sore tits. "The ideas he gets, and the birds he's fucked. It can't be for real, no girl would go with a strange man and fuck like that, would she?"

"No darling," I murmured. "I must have a bath first, then we'll go to bed."

I never went back to Barry James's office, which was a pity. I've read many of his books now, and I'd like to try some more of his ideas out. Still, you never know, do you?

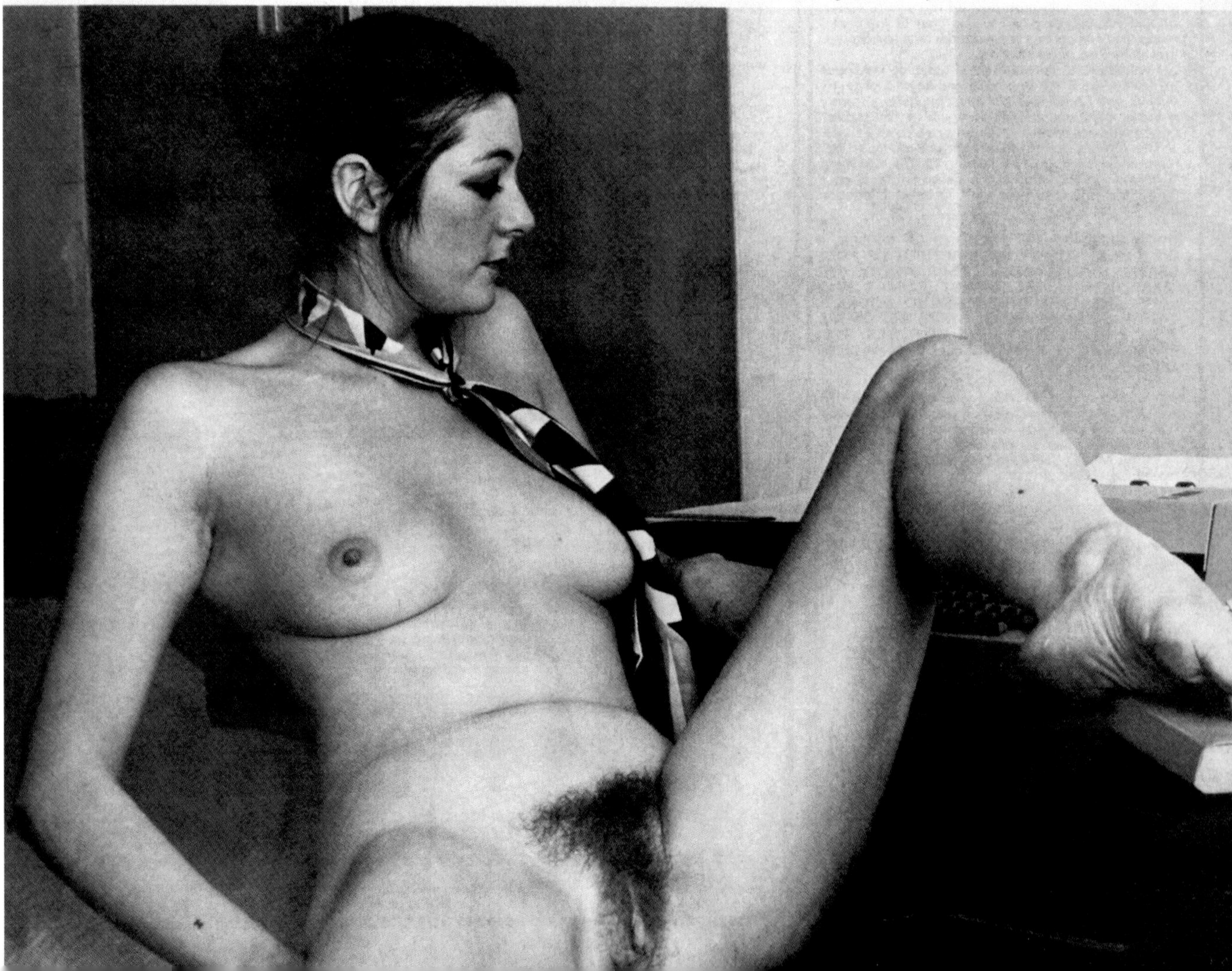

The Cheerful Scapegoat (We Three)

Wayne Koestenbaum

You published a new book, *Transplantations Medical.* We discussed the odd title. The word 'transplantations' recalled your painful emigration to this country, and the plantations shadowing our immoral nation's history. *Transplantations Medical,* like *Paradise Lost,* put the noun before the adjective. 'The lost paradise of the medical transplantation', I suggested, fixing the inversion - but already you were angry and confused.

You'd suffered medical injuries, wounds I was incapable of discussing with sufficient empathy; and so you urged me to discontinue the conversation.

I persisted. I wanted to discuss transsexual existences. Everything I'd ever felt or seen could fall under the category of 'transsexual' - but then the classification system, which had promised momentarily to comprehend me, faltered, if a system can falter...

On top of the hill a new rest home opened. Different existences, stacked on top of each other - or do I mean 'different bodies'? - opened to my curious fingers. 'A home can't open to fingers', I said, hoping that you would pull all copies of *Transplantations Medical* from the shelves, and rewrite the book, and include a new chapter, discussing my fingers and their preternatural capacity to open new rest homes on hilltops.

You and I drove to the waterfront. One texture rose to the fore - a nubbiness I couldn't explain. I sank away from the possibility of explanation, and tried instead to touch your summer jacket's cottony protuberances.

You'd dedicated *Transplantations Medical* to me - a benediction I didn't deserve, though it enlarged my sway. Because you were a best-selling writer translated into twenty-four languages, readers around the globe would discover me, ponder my existence, fantasize about my body. Clever interpreters would understand that my physique's peculiarity, which shall go undescribed, was one of the transplantations cited in the title.

You masturbated, then, in front of me, as we sat on a bench overlooking the harbor. Perhaps you weren't masturbating; perhaps you were simply lodging a complaint against yourself, and the complaint took the form of finger-play. I turned away, to give you privacy; I considered returning to the bar and ordering a lobster roll. We could split the roll, after you had finished your distracting episode of self-stimulation - whether a hobby or a livelihood, I couldn't discern.

You weren't nude, though you were investigating your body with repeated, subtle motions. I alternated between watching your investigation and watching what passed for 'activity' on the bay. This activity consisted of three night-crawling boats, small and perhaps not navigated by humans. The boats were evenly spaced, never overlapping, but the middle boat seemed to wish to speed ahead of the others.

'Fellow animals', said a man, startling us. 'May I share this bench of happenstance with you?' He urged his body between ours. We made way for him, and let his corpulence bisect our comity.

'Slate', you said. 'Dear Slate'. You embraced him. You'd met in the hospital, after your trolley accident. Slate had been visiting his sister, who was also a patient in the emergency room. He befriended you, returned to see you every day of your hospitalization, watched your swellings subside and your contusions heal. As you recovered, a romance blossomed, watered by pity.

On Slate's nose, a flap of skin seemed ready to disengage, as if he, too, had been subject to transplantations. I felt an impulse to tug at the flap, to complete its process of lazy migration away from the nose proper.

You noticed the flap and tore it off. Slate screamed, and then laughed. 'Good riddance', he said. 'I'd meant to ask a dermatologist to complete the refiguration'.

'Last call for lobster rolls', I said. I offered to buy one for us to share; I would ask the bartender to split it into equal portions.

The bartender told me that she was out of lobster. Would pike suffice? She cut the roll into thirds.

'Pike', said Slate, when I explained the substitution, 'takes me back to childhood, before I was what you suburban clods call a "bum". In the summer, Dad and I would go fishing. We'd drive to the bridge, and cast our poles over the edge. Then a superhighway project came along, and the community didn't put up a fight. Fishing opportunities dwindled. Dad lost his job at the accounting firm, started drinking, grew violent. I began turning tricks, as revenge. Dad wanted me to save myself for marriage. Wedlock, I believed, was rot - a pious sewage system. I had no intention of corraling myself into dead arrangements. I flouted Dad and the law, but the law pursued me. Three years in prison - and then, a hardscrabble life on the streets. Slowly I climbed back to bookishness'.

You turned to me and explained, 'In the emergency room, Slate kept vigil over my bed'.

'And when you got out of the hospital', Slate continued, 'I helped you with manual composition. I didn't mind not being credited as co-author. I contributed only a few paragraphs per chapter'.

I watched the three boats on the bay. They were approaching the lighthouse, its signal pulsating, as if issuing a decree. Who could figure out whether the signal was hopeful or pessimistic?

I wanted desperately to be included in the story Slate was telling about your relationship's sordid prehistory, but I also feared the consequences of Slate discovering that you had dedicated *Transplantations Medical* to me. I was a good enough judge of character to intuit that Slate might be willing to maim me as punishment for stealing the limelight.

The three of us woke the next morning in your bed: a car alarm, on the street, ruptured our sleep. In the middle of the night, we'd each suffered food poisoning, a mild case, not so dire that it interfered with our nascent, tripartite intimacy. One by one we'd risen from bed to do our business in the lavatory - then back to sleep for a few dehydrated hours.

That afternoon we visited the new rest home on the hill. Preliminary research, you said, in preparation for your next book, the sequel to *Transplantations Medical*. Cognitive enfeeblement would be the new volume's subject.

Slate agreed to take a job at the rest home, as mole, to do undercover research. I volunteered to write empirical paragraphs, as usual, to bolster your book's grasp on the veritable. Facts came easily to me. You specialized in ghosts, predictions, epiphenomena. Your authority in matters figmental spread your reputation around the globe. Buried within the speculations were the facts I subserviently pilfered for your sake, from sources as various as park benches and harbor vistas.

One morning, late in the sequel's composition, I looked deeply into Slate's eyes. No trace of the nose refiguration remained visible. Slate's nose was large, but only in profile. As I stared into his eyes, his nose seemed to diminish in size and importance. My sexual relationship with Slate had intensified; your body had never appealed to me, and as the cognitive enfeeblement project evolved, your impoverished imagination and remorseless judgments soured me on the prospect of ever embracing you again. I would consent to sit beside you while you investigated your own body with strange half-indiscernible movements of wrist and fingers, but I wouldn't participate. Into Slate's eyes, however, I could contentedly gaze with a sense of nostalgia for the father who didn't approve of Slate's early career as hustler. The 'Dad' of Slate's narration grew more palpable to me, as Slate held me in his rough arms. The 'Dad' of Slate's narration, no longer a weekend fisherman, no longer a son-bruiser, now only a suggestion of flannel shirts and flexed dorsal muscles, thickened into more than figment, as I surrendered to Slate's caresses. You would not have called it surrender. You, more intellectually adept, would have found a frostier word. I would like you to describe Slate's attachment to my body, his style of making my body his own. How would you depict the regularity or fitfulness of his thrusts, shoves, and adhesions?

Slate claimed amnesia. 'I blacked out', he said. 'I lost track of my hands. Was I touching you, or touching myself? Or were my hands not involved in our lonely yet overpopulated congress?'

Occasional opened windows in the rest home admitted nearby sounds of revelers, with their guitars, tambourines, cymbals, and kettle-drums. From the hill, one could look down upon the town and the harbor. The revelers arrived and departed without a schedule; whenever I had the good fortune of visiting Slate in the rest home, while he was engaged in undercover research, I savored the unannounced sounds of mallets striking drum-skins. Would you include these sounds in your sequel? I will ask you tonight. I wish I could claim loyalty to a cause ethically keener than your sequel or those unseen drums - but Slate has quashed my idealism. The scar on his stomach - a knife-wound he won't explain - remains red and raised. You could make it vanish if you were omnipotent, but you suffer, as do I, from truncated vision. Shake-clatter-shake went the tambourine outside the rest-home window as Slate kissed me, a kiss that would, I hope, undo my subservience to sound and to sequel.

Slate's phallus unnaturally tapered at its head. That was not my favorite genital configuration. I told him so. You felt otherwise. You savored the pointy kind. You called it 'rare, not porcine'. To it - the pointiness - I applied my usual straightforwardness. I handled it, the end and the beginning, with a docility almost ductile in its willingness to stay away from the higher frequencies of rage. To the whims of Slate's pointiness I cheerfully hearkened, with hand and mouth and any other aspect of my physique that I could muster. My capacities for mustering were limited, fabulously so. You indicted me for these limitations, and, later, wrote about the indictment. Again and again you and I would sit on the harbor bench and discuss my limitations.

From Freud's antiquities collection

Sigmund Freud

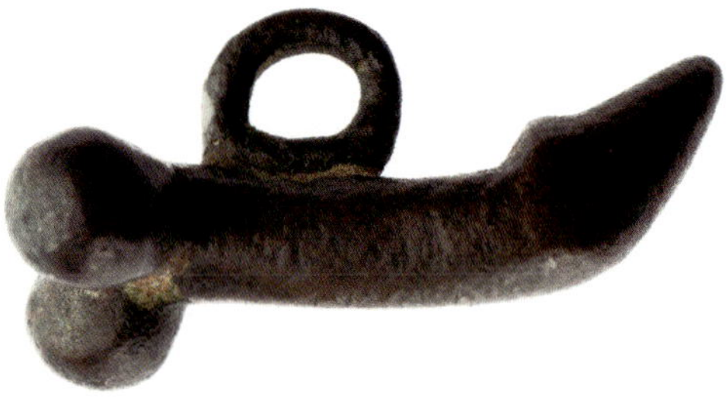

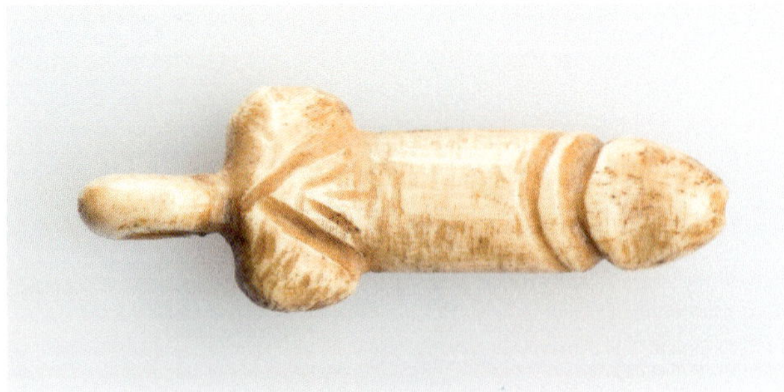

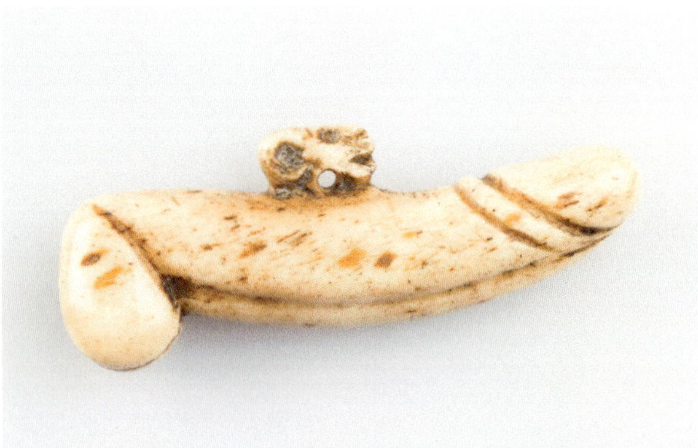

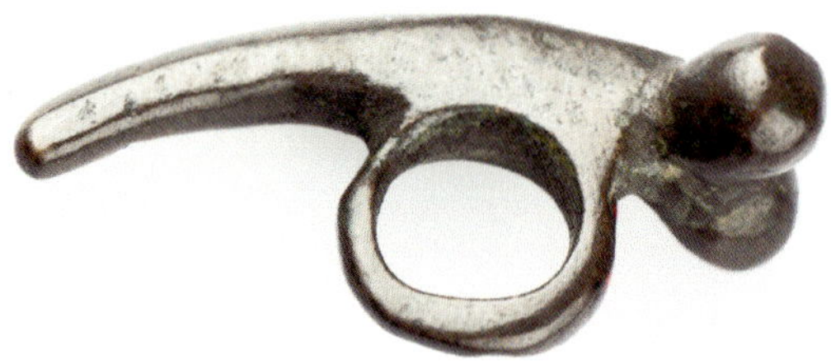

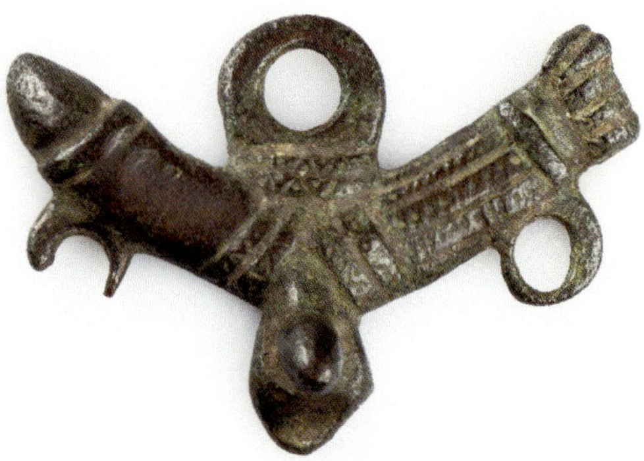

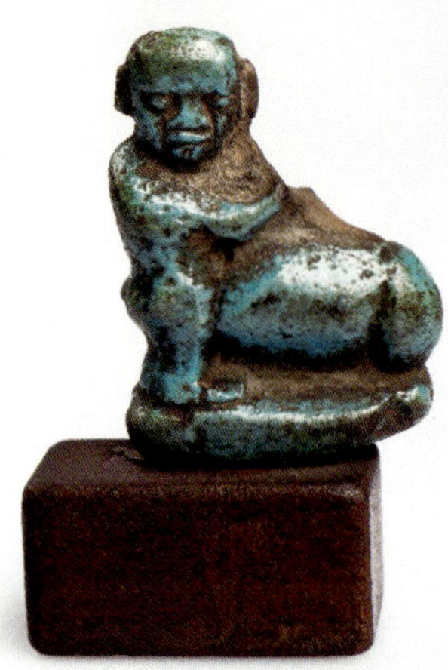

Image Credits

VALIE EXPORT
Pages 11-13, Stills from *Mann & Frau & Animal*
Courtesy of sixpackfilm.

Chantal Faust
Page 21, *Für Laura*, 2015

Emma Talbot
Pages 26-27, *SEX FANTASY*
Size: 94 cm x 63 cm
gouache on Japanese paper
Courtesy of Emma Talbot & Petra Rinck Galerie

Michelle Williams Gamaker
Pages 37-41, Video stills from *Neophytes* (2018), 3-channel HD video

Shannon Bell
Page 45, Illustration by Suzann Gage in *A New View of a Woman's Body*
Pages 54, 57, 62, Stills from film *Nice Girls Don't Do It*. Image Shannon Bell, filmmaker Kath Daymond
Pages 47-49, issue of *Rites* Mag. Images Shannon Bell, Photographer RuthAnn Tucker

Antony Gormley
Page 66, *CONCEPTION*, 1989
Blood and semen on paper
31 x 40 cm

Jordan Mckenzie
Pages 69-71, *Spent* 2009: artist's semen, universal litmus paper
(Photographer Alessandra Ferrini)

Annie Sprinkle and Beth Stephens
Pages 80-84, *We Made Love With Marcel Duchamp*
1. *R. Muff*

2. *L.H.O.O.Q.*
3. *The Love Handle*
plus ephemera

Charan Singh
Page 93, *Untitled,* from the series *Garden of Eros,* India, 2016

Cosey Fanni Tutti
Pages 94-102, *The Office Cleaner*
Supersex No.8
1975-1976
Courtesy Cabinet London and the artist

Robert Pruzan
Page 75, *Scott O'Hara in the Powerhouse Greasy Jockstrap Contest, San Francisco* (1985)
Courtesy of Gay, Lesbian, Bisexual, Transgender Historical Society

Collection of Sigmund Freud
Page 108
Phallus, Roman, bronze
LDFRD 4144

Two ivory phallic amulets with a loop, Japanese, Ivory, 19th century
LDFRD 3408/9

Phallic amulet with hanging loop, Roman, bronze
LDFRD 3499

Fist and Phallus amulet, Roman, Bronze
LDFRD 3392

Ithyphallic Figure, Egyptian, Late Period 715BC-332BC, faience
LDFRD 3776

Biographical Notes

Shannon Bell is Professor of Political Science at York University, Toronto, Canada (http://www.yorku.ca/shanbell/). Her books include: *Fast Feminism* (2010), *Reading, Writing and Rewriting the Prostitute Body* (1994), *Whore Carnival* (1995), *Bad Attitude/s on Trial co-authored* (1997, republished 2017);*The Book of Radical General Semantics*, co-edited (2016), *Subversive Itinerary: The Thought of Gad Horowitz*, co-edited (2013) and *New Socialisms*, co-edited (2004).

Lee Edelman is Fletcher Professor of English Literature at Tufts University. Publications include *No Future: Queer Theory and the Death Drive* (Duke University Press, 2004), *Homographesis: Essays in Gay Literary and Cultural Theory* (Routledge, 1993), and *Transmemberment of Song: Hart Crane's Anatomies of Rhetoric and Desire* (Stanford, 1987)

VALIE EXPORT is an Austrian artist. Her artistic work includes video installations, body performances, expanded cinema, computer animations, photography, sculptures and publications covering contemporary arts. Her work is included in international private and public collections including that of the Centre Pompidou, Paris, Tate Modern, London, Reina Sophia, Madrid, MoMA, New York, and MoCA, Los Angeles.

Chantal Faust is an artist, writer and Senior Tutor in Critical & Historical Studies and Research in the School of Arts & Humanities at the Royal College of Art.

Antony Gormley is widely acclaimed for his sculptures, installations and public artworks that investigate the relationship of the human body to space. His best known works include the *Angel of the North*, a public sculpture in Gateshead in the North of England, commissioned in 1994 and erected in 1998, *Another Place* on Crosby Beach near Liverpool (1997), and *Event Horizon*, a multi-part site installation which premiered in London in 2007, around Madison Square in New York City in 2010, in São Paulo, Brazil, in 2012, and in Hong Kong in 2015–16. Gormley's work has been exhibited throughout the UK and internationally with recent exhibitions at Hall Art Foundation in Germany (2017-18), Long Museum in Shanghai (2017) and National Portrait Gallery in London (2016).

Lois Keidan is the Co-Director of the Live Art Development Agency (LADA) which she co-founded in 1999. From 1992 to 1997 she was Director of Live Arts at the ICA, London. Prior to that she was responsible for Performance Art at Arts Council of England, and previously worked at the Midland Group, Nottingham and Theatre Workshop, Edinburgh.

Wayne Koestenbaum has published nineteen books of poetry, criticism, and fiction, including *Notes on Glaze, The Pink Trance Notebooks, My 1980s & Other Essays, Hotel Theory, Best-Selling Jewish Porn Films, Andy Warhol, Humiliation, Jackie Under My Skin,* and *The Queen's Throat* (a National Book Critics Circle Award finalist). His newest book of poetry, *Camp Marmalade,* appeared in 2018. He has exhibited his paintings in solo shows at White Columns (New York), 356 Mission (L.A.), and the University of Kentucky Art Museum. His first piano/vocal record, *Lounge Act,* was released by Ugly Duckling Presse Records in 2017; he has given musical performances at The Kitchen, REDCAT, Centre Pompidou, The Walker Art Center, and the Renaissance Society. He is a Distinguished Professor of English, Comparative Literature, and French at the CUNY Graduate Center in New York City.

Dominic Johnson is Reader in Performance and Visual Culture in the School of English and Drama at Queen Mary University of London. He is the author of *Glorious Catastrophe: Jack Smith, Performance and Visual Culture* (2012), *Theatre & the Visual* (2012); and *The Art of Living: An Oral History of Performance Art* (2015). He is the editor of five books, including most recently *Pleading in the Blood: The Art and Performances of Ron Athey* (2013); and (with Deirdre Heddon) *It's All Allowed: The Performances of Adrian Howells* (2016). He is also an Editor of the journal *Contemporary Theatre Review.*

Thomas W. Laqueur is Helen Fawcett Professor of History at University of California Berkeley. His publications include *The Work of the Dead: A Cultural History of Mortal Remains* (2015) *Solitary Sex: A Cultural History of Masturbation* (2003), and *Making Sex: Body and Gender from the Greeks to Freud* (1990).

Jordan McKenzie is a performance maker/visual artist and academic based in London. Research interests include queerness and identity, presentations of class in contemporary Britain and the intersections of social housing, arts practices and socially situated art. He has exhibited both nationally and internationally in galleries, festivals and arts centers including Freud Museum (2015); Yorkshire Sculpture Park (2014); KASA Gallery, Istanbul (2014); Arnolfini Gallery (2011); Courtauld Institute (2011). His curatorial projects include LUPA (Lock Up Performance Art) a performance space run from a disused garage on the council estate where he lives in East London, co-curated with Aaron Williamson and Kate Mahony (2011-13); Look At The (E)state We're In, a major international conference about art and the council estate (2014); Live(E)lseWhere (co-curated with The Drawing Shed 2014). He has received major arts bursaries and awards from Arts Council England, Arts Admin and The Live Art Development Agency and been an artist-in-residence in numerous countries including I-Park Massachusetts, USA (2012), OVADA Gallery, Oxford (2005) and Sutra Arts, Nepal (2004).

He is currently a lecturer in Drawing at The University for the Arts, London and an academic support lecturer at Wimbledon College of Art, UAL.

Susie Orbach is a psychotherapist, psychoanalyst, and social critic. She is the author of many books. Her latest *In Therapy: The Unfolding Story* is an expanded edition of *In Therapy* (an annotated version of the BBC series listened to live by 2 million people). Her first book *Fat is a Feminist Issue* has been continuously in print since 1978. She was recently the recipient of the first Lifetime Achievement Award from the British Psychoanalytical Society.

Emily Pope is an artist based in London. She makes t-shirts, bags, audio and is currently making a sitcom called *The Sitcom Show*. She also writes and reads. Recent exhibitions & projects include: NOQ, The Royal Standard Liverpool, ASP, ICA London; Feral Kin, Auto Italia, London; The Court Summons, Ladette Space, London; Tarantellegra, Hester, New York; and together with Ruth Angel Edwards: *Got 2 B*, a radio show on Resonance FM. It seems she has now been kicked off the radio, which may be her own fault due to abysmal timekeeping and swearing on air, so she has archived the project on the internet. She has a masters in Critical Writing from the Royal College of Art, and studied at the School of the Damned, a free postgraduate art course run by and for its students.

Adrian Rifkin works with film and cinema, classical and popular music, canonical art and mass imagery, literature and pornography. His publications include *Communards and Other Cultural Histories* (with Steve Edwards, 2018), *Ingres Then, and Now* (1999), *Street Noises* (1993), and his essays have been collected in *Interdisciplinary Encounters: Hidden and Visible Explorations of the Work of Adrian Rifkin* (edited by Dana Arnold, 2014). Adrian is Visiting Professor at Central Saint Martins, University of the Arts London, and many of his writings can be found here: http://gai-savoir.net

Charan Singh, lives and works in New Delhi and London. Singh's research and practice is informed by HIV/AIDS work and community activism in India. His work revisits his 'pre-English language' life, and is looking at languages, landscapes, legitimacies, and explores importance of storytelling, role of translation. He is a PhD candidate at the Royal College of Art, London. He was an artist resident at the FIAR, New York, July 2017. His most recent published work is 'Delhi: Communities of Belonging', The New Press 2016; with Sunil Gupta. His latest exhibition is at the Contemporary Art Museum Houston, 'Dissent and Desire' (catalogue), January - April, 2018, and previously exhibited at SepiaEye, New York 2017. He earned a Magnum/Photo London award in 2016 for his portrait series 'Kothis, Hijras, Giriyas and Others', that was also shown in 'I am a Camera' at FotoFest Houston and The

Photographer's Gallery, London 2015. This series is featured in the Photoworks Annual, UK 2017. His work is in several private collections.

Dr Marquard Smith is an academic, curator, Founder and Editor-in-Chief of *Journal of Visual Culture*, and Program Leader for the MA Museums & Galleries in Education at UCL Institute of Education, London. As a curator, Marq's exhibitions include 'Blood & Bones' (The Street Gallery, UCLH, forthcoming 2018), 'Solitary Pleasures' (Freud Museum, 2018), 'How to Construct a Time Machine' (2014), 'The Global Archive' (2012), and 'How We Became Metadata' (2010). He's written on the art, visual, material, and immaterial culture of 'the human' in capitalist modernity, and publications include *The Erotic Doll* (Yale University Press, 2014), *The Prosthetic Impulse* (co-edited, The MIT Press, 2005), *Stelarc: The Monograph* (The MIT Press, 2005), and *The Prosthetic Aesthetic* (co-edited, *New Formations*, 2002). Marq is embarking on a new project entitled 'Human Resources', on the futures (and histories) of 'the human' as a bio-informational resource.

Beth Stephens & **Annie Sprinkle** live and work together in the redwood forest of Boulder Creek and in an old Victorian cottage in San Francisco. Devoted to pollinating the ecosex movement through art, theory, practice and activism since 2004, they've produced numerous performance art works, ecosex symposiums, weddings to nature entities, workshops, walking tours, and art exhibits. Their award winning documentary, *Goodbye Gauley Mountain: An Ecosexual Love Story* played many film festivals and is on iTunes. Beth is an Art Professor at UC Santa Cruz, Annie was the first porn star to earn a Ph.D. They were official documenta14 artists (2017) where their new film, *Water Makes Us Wet - An Ecosexual Adventure* premiered. They co-authored *Explorer's Guide to Planet Orgasm - For Every Body* published by Greenery Press (2017) and currently they're completing a book about their work, *Assuming the Ecosexual Position* for University of Minnesota Press. They both love masturbation.

Emma Talbot is an artist who lives and works in London. She is represented by Petra Rinck Galerie Düsseldorf and Galerie Onrust Amsterdam. She works closely with Arcadia Missa London/NYC and Nicolas Krupp Galerie Basel. Recent one person exhibitions include: *Woman-Snake-Bird,* Galerie Onrust Amsterdam (2018), *Open Thoughts*, Never Aachener Kunstverein, Germany (2017), *The World Blown Apart*, Galerie Onrust, Amsterdam (2017), *Stained With Marks Of Love*, Arcadia Missa, NYC (2017), *Time After Time*, Petra Rinck Galerie, Düsseldorf (2016), and *Unravel These Knots*, Freud Museum London (2016). Recent group exhibitions include: *Journeys With The Waste Land*, Turner Contemporary Margate (2018), *Virginia Woolf*, Tate St Ives (2018, touring to Pallant House Gallery, Fitzwilliam Museum), *CONDO*, Arcadia Missa, London (2017), *MAC International Ulster Bank Prize*, MAC Belfast (2016), *Ghost On A Wire*, Objectifs

Centre for Photography and Film, Singapore (2016), *John Moores Painting Prize*, Walker Art Gallery, Liverpool (2016), *Comic Tragics*, Art Gallery of Western Australia, Perth (2016). Emma's work has been reviewed and featured in *Frieze, Flash Art, ArtReview, Frankfurter Allgemeine Zeitung, Kunstforum, Der Groene Amsterdammer & The Guardian* and is held in major collections including The David Roberts Collection UK, AGWA, Perth, AUS, Freis Museum NL, Arnhem Museum NL, KRC Collection NL, Birmingham Museum and Art Gallery, UK. Emma is a Tutor in the Painting Programme at the Royal College of Art.

Locating her activity within the arena of the sex industry, the individual Magazine Actions casts **Cosey Fanni Tutti** in myriad roles according to various scenarios designed for the arousal of male readers. The magazines in their entirety index a peculiarly erogenous zone of English society, distilling absurd sexual fantasies through photography, prose, satirical cartoons, advertisements and disparate headline typography. Cosey's modeling career was one facet of a wider artistic remit which involved her concurrently in the work of Coum Transmissions and the prototypical industrial group Throbbing Gristle. Common to all manifestations is a highly personal and mediated form of performance. No hierarchy of meaning was applied within the totality of Cosey's practice. This enabled the agile migration of her live actions from the sex industry to the equally reified context of the art world. In the 1976 exhibition 'PROSTITUTION', staged at the I.C.A, London within the collective efforts of Coum Transmissions, Cosey's singular acts of exposure proposed an exchange of apparently prohibitive currency; one that challenged the social and economic constructs of two industries in which Cosey had elected to work - art and sex. The press acted as an essential stimulus; daily cuttings in response to the show taken from broadsheets and tabloids alike were incorporated into the I.C.A exhibition. The censorial relegation of the nude photographs extracted from sex magazines to white boxes epitomised an institutional dichotomy but more crucially catalysed the very agents that were to accelerate her image according to the multiple personalities adopted by and conferred upon Cosey. Cosey's professional engagement with the commercial sex industry positioned her *contraposto* to the prevailing didactic explorations of gender politics favoured by her female contemporaries. If this was an energetic problematic in the late Seventies, then Cosey's current practice is concerned with the reframing of past experience in relation to the present, as in her audio-visual self-portrait *Harmonic COUMaction* (2017) and her recent autobiography *Art Sex Music* (Faber & Faber, 2017).

Ivan Ward is Deputy Director and Head of Learning at the Freud Museum London and manager of the Museum's acclaimed conference programme. He is the author of a number of books and papers on psychoanalytic theory and on the applications of psychoanalysis to social and cultural issues. His latest publication is '*Parsifal* as Castration Drama' (2017) included in a special issue of *The Wagner Journa*l based on a conference organised by the Freud Museum in 2016.

Michelle Williams Gamaker is a London-based artist working with moving image and performance. Her latest project is *The Eternal Return* (2019), the third film in a trilogy that explores the idea of brown protagonists. Recent films include *The Fruit is There to be Eaten*(2018) and *House of Women* (2017) revisionist restagings of British directors Powell & Pressburger's female characters in *Black Narcissus*(1947). Recent screenings include Transmediale, Berlin and BFI Flare 2018: London LGBT+ Film Festival. Current shows include 'History Repeats Itself' at MIMA Middlesbrough Institute of Modern Art and she is co-curator (with Nick Norton) and lead artist of 'Library Interventions: Moving Knowledge' in Leeds Art Gallery. Alongside her moving image work she has two feature films in development: 'The Imperial' and 'Violet Culbo' (with Film London (FLAMIN) and the Cross Channel Film Lab). Michelle is also a Lecturer in BA Fine Art at Goldsmiths College, University of London, Chair of Trustees at Pavilion in Leeds, and co-founder of the Women of Colour Index (WOCI) Reading Group with Samia Malik and Rehana Zaman.

Acknowledgements
Marquard Smith

Many thanks to: Marina Abramovic; Maria Acconci; Giuliano Argenziano, Polly Mukai-Heidt, Allison Brainard, Sydney Fishman, and Theus Zwakhals at the Marina Abramoviæ Institute and LIMA distributor; Matthew Barney; Samira Ben at *Extra Extra*; Josephine Borradaile; Brigitte Bourguelot at Galerie Beaubourg; Andrew Brown at Art/Books; Lesley Burgess; Brittany Crosby at the Erotic Heritage Museum in Las Vegas; Oliver Carruthers at Richmix; Giulia Casalini at Richard Saltoun Gallery; Alfie Chubb; David Cunningham; Bryony Davies, Stefan Marianski, Jamie Ruers, Lili Spain, and Karolina Urbaniak at the Freud Museum; Stuart Frost, Philip Attwood, Freddie Matthews, and Bryony Smith the British Museum; The Freud Museum's Contemporary Art Committee and its Trustees; Maria Fusco; Hoss Ghonouie at the Everyman Cinema; Sigrid Guggenberger at Atelier VALIE EXPORT; Katalin-Tüende Huber, Marjeta Jerne, and Elisabeth Freudensprung at the Austrian Cultural Forum London; Veljko Jelenkoviæ at the Embassy of the Republic of Serbia in London; Travis Jeppesen; Tom Jones; Ky at SH!; Tom Laycock at Honour; Finn Love and Alex Eisenberg at the Live Art Development Agency; Elizabeth Lynch; Jenni Lomax (then) at Camden Arts Centre; Jamie Maclean at the *Erotic Review*; Olga Makhroff at Centre Pompidou; Oliver Meek at the Rio Dalston; Julia Michalska at theartnewspaper; Bryony McLennan and Laura Peterle at Antony Gormley Studio; Heinz Neumann; Sally O'Reilly; Isabelle Piechaczyk at Sixpackfilm; Sian Putnam; Vivian Rehberg; Lauren Smith, Rosie Motley, and Allyson Spellacy at the Gladstone Gallery and Atelier Matthew Barney; Andres Serrano, Irina Serrano, Ilaria Tortora, and Marion Adrian, and Constance Dumas at Galerie Nathalie Obadia; Mark Snyder (then) at the Museum of Sex in New York; Jeffrey Storer at the Leather Archives & Museum in Chicago; and Andrew Wheatley at CABINET London.

I'm-*so-incredibly-grateful-to*: Shannon Bell, David Bennett, Liz Bentley, Sean Curran, Lee Edelman, VALIE EXPORT, Sarah H. Forbes, Johnny Golding, Antony Gormley, Natika H Halil, Dominic Johnson, Malja Kaunisto, Thomas W. Laqueur, Jordan McKenzie, David Morgan, Michael Newman, Susie Orbach, Emily Pope, Adrian Rifkin, Charan Singh, Beth Stephens & Annie Sprinkle, Emma Talbot, Esther Teichmann, Cosey Fanni Tutti, Michelle Williams Gamaker, and Wayne Koestenbaum.

There-are-not-the-words-to-even-begin-to-express-my-gratitude to: Lois Keidan and CJ Mitchell at the Live Art Development Agency; Chantal Faust; Vanessa Fewster at the Austrian Cultural Forum London; Mark Little; Joanne Morra; Florence Schechter at the Vagina Museum; and Carol Seigel, Ivan Ward, and Lizzie Glendinning at the Freud Museum.

FREUD MUSEUM LONDON

austrian cultural forum lon

Royal College of Art

THE BOOK CLUB

VAGINA MUSEUM

THE ARCHIVES GALLERY

LADA

Live Art Development Agency